EARLY PRAISE FOR
CARRIED BY FAITH...

"From the first paragraph t~ ~~ memoir is raw and intriguir stop reading it — a true ex "

— Lisa Plc ~~n of the ELCA

"Every interaction w~~ ~ue is filled with a refreshing hope that's rooted in her miraculous story, which has God's fingerprints all over it. Be encouraged in your own journey."

— **Danita Bye, Author,** *Millennials Matter: Proven Strategies for Building Your Next Gen Leader*

"Sue lets you experience her struggle with substance abuse and her transparency lets you witness how the Holy Spirit has used her as a messenger, an angel with skin. Hopeful, honest and inspiring. Thank you for sharing your courageous story."

— **Sally Brown**

"With brutal honesty, Sue tells the gripping and inspiring story of breaking out of her prison of addiction. You will experience the anger, anxiety and confusion of Sue and her family in the pages of this book. But in the end, your heart will be warmed."

— **Janice Krohn, Regional Speaker,
Trainer – Stonecroft**

"As the reader, you can feel Sue's authentic self coming forward in every chapter. Her faith and tenacity are inspiring!"

— Kim Berning, RN, BSN, MSN

"It left me feeling uplifted because it gave me hope; it encouraged, knowing she overcame so much and I could do it too; it comforted, knowing that I am not alone in this journey; and it enlightened by the way she displays her ever-constant faith in her God! A true testament to God's forgiveness and all-encompassing love! A good insight of what it was like, what happened and what it's like now!"

— Mary Schaefer

"Sue's transparency is shared in her life's story. *Carried by Faith* gives hope to the hopeless and ministers healing to those who have been deeply wounded on the journey. Truly a testimony of God's "continued" faithfulness to mankind regardless of what season we may be in, confirming our purpose here on earth."

— Pastor Larry Borud, Northland Harvest Church

"I was captivated from the moment I picked the book up. The message of hope, healing and reconciliation in Jesus Christ is refreshing and needed in today's culture."

— Pastor Rhonda Rice

"*Carried by Faith* is a descriptive, vivid and honest account of the impact of substance abuse and addiction. The untold story that finds its way between the pages is the unwavering and faithful hope of family and friends. This story of struggle fills us with hope when faith wins out. Through the reality of a miracle, a new road is traveled that is filled with meaning and purpose. We can best touch the lives of others when we have been to those places where others find themselves. *Carried by Faith* is such a story and proves once again that when the days look the darkest, God is nearby waiting for our outstretched arms.

— **Pastor Gerald Roise**

Eph 3:20-21

20 Now to Him who is able to do
~~really~~ exceedingly abundantly beyond
all that we ask, imagine or dream of,
according to the power that works in us,
21 to Him be the glory in the church and in
Christ Jesus throughout all generations,
forever and ever. Amen

Happy Birthday Carole 5-26-18
Eph 3:20-21
God's richest blessings on your day!

Sue L. Hamilton

CARRIED

BY

Faith

From
SUBSTANCE ABUSE
to a Life Filled with
MIRACLES

A Memoir

LIVE4ONE ENTERPRISE LLC | MINOT, ND

Live4One Enterprise LLC
P.O. Box 1425
Minot, ND 58702
www.live4oneenterprise.com

Scripture quotations marked (NIV) are taken from the Holy Bible, New International Version®, NIV®. Copyright © 1973, 1978, 1984, 2011 by Biblica, Inc.™ Used by permission of Zondervan. All rights reserved worldwide. www.zondervan.com The "NIV" and "New International Version" are trademarks registered in the United States Patent and Trademark Office by Biblica, Inc.™

Scripture quotations marked (NLT) are taken from the Holy Bible, New Living Translation, copyright © 1996, 2004, 2007 by Tyndale House Foundation. Used by permission of Tyndale House Publishers, Inc., Carol Stream, Illinois 60188. All rights reserved.

Scripture quotations marked CSB have been taken from the Christian Standard Bible®, Copyright © 2017 by Holman Bible Publishers. Used by permission. Christian Standard Bible® and CSB® are federally registered trademarks of Holman Bible Publishers.

Scripture quotations marked MSG are taken from THE MESSAGE, copyright © 1993, 1994, 1995, 1996, 2000, 2001, 2002 by Eugene H. Peterson. Used by permission of NavPress. All rights reserved. Represented by Tyndale House Publishers, Inc.

ISBN: 978-0-9993634-0-9

Library of Congress Control Number: 2017917013

Printed in the United States of America

DEDICATION

To Mom

You loved me unconditionally through thick and thin. You were patient, loving, and always waiting for me. This shows what an accepting, kind, and tolerant person you are.

You always provided nice things for me, encouraged me, and helped me with anything I needed. You had the strength and determination to never give up on me. You had eternal hope that I would come out on the other side. For that, I am forever grateful!

You also taught me several practical things that I have carried through my life. You taught me to get up every day like you have somewhere to go; to get up, get dressed and look good, even if you do not leave the house. You showed me to pick up the house and make everything look nice and neat, even if no one else will be coming over. And, the one skill you never instructed me to do, but showed me through being a great example, was to make others feel special by remembering their birthday with a card or small gift.

I know now the agony I put you through as a mother. As a grateful daughter, I recognize the many things you did for me. You may have thought I would never remember your many actions that impacted me, but I do.

- You loved my strong-willed, independent personality.
- You loved me and didn't hate me.
- You always had hope for me when others gave up on me.
- You continually prayed for me when others had tossed my future out the window.
- You forgave me when I could not forgive myself.
- You tolerated my lifestyle, actions, and consequences.
- You continued to show me affection by hugging me when I repeatedly pushed you away. You knew the protective walls I built would eventually be broken down.
- Perfect example of "tough love."

Thank you for being so strong, for not giving up, and for waiting patiently for God's work to be done.

I am truly sorry for the years of pain I put you through. Thank you for standing by me through all those crazy years of my life. I know, without any doubt, I would not be where I am today if it were not for your loving prayers. The prayers and your faith got me through while God carried me in the wilderness. I love you very much! *Thank you, Mom!*

To Dad

I know it is difficult for you to hear the words "I love you" face to face. So, I will express my words on paper. I want you to know some important things and how much you have taught me through my life.

* You taught me a strong work ethic: to never give up, to not be afraid, and to keep pushing on when you feel you cannot push anymore.

* You taught me a keen business sense and how to treat a customer well.

* You taught me how to sell most anything — pigeon seed, Mason shoes, and mini-donuts.

* You taught me to keep knocking on doors even when they get shut in my face.

* You taught me to have an "eagle eye" and look at the details in all projects.

* You taught me how to never get lost by teaching me techniques of using landmarks and constantly being aware of physical surroundings so to keep my directional compass set.

* You taught me to stand up for what I believe.

I have *always* loved you. No matter what you have said to me or thought about me, *I love you, no matter what!*

CONTENTS

PREFACE

My life is not unique, yet God has given me the ability to share how *He* found me when I was "hiding" from Him. Many times, only the horrible life stories are shared by feeling the need to justify things that have gone wrong and to point fingers and accuse others. There are many things in my life I wish were different, memories of the past; good, bad, funny, and sad, which all helped me to understand who I am today.

I look at my life as a work of God's hand molding me into the true person He wants me to be. He has written a story for me, just as He has written one for you.

My goal is for you to relate to me, to know there are others who have walked in your shoes, to know you are not alone. It is a freeing experience when you can find hope and know there is another way to live.

In this book, you will read little stories amongst the *big* story. The *big* story is God saving my life and using it to touch others' lives and sharing how He has allowed me to survive so I can live and love Him with all my heart.

God worked in my life even when I was "hiding" from Him and destroying it. The story is about how God used me as an earthen vessel. God created a miracle out of my life, carried me and saved me from my dark past into a life worth living!

To each of you, I pray the story God created in me gives you hope, inspiration, and love.

INTRODUCTION

My self-will ran rampant through my young years of life. During that time, I was determined to stay "in control" and let no one else control me. This led to years of isolation, fear, and many harmful situations. I flirted with the enemy, Satan, for many years as I tried to stay "in control." Many times, darkness nearly engulfed me as Satan tried to destroy me. Unbeknownst to me, God always "had my back" and was carrying me and protecting my entire life.

For you created my inmost being;
you knit me together in my mother's womb.
I praise you because I am fearfully
and wonderfully made;
your works are wonderful,
I know that full well.
My frame was not hidden from you when
I was made in the secret place.

When I was woven together in the depths of the earth,
your eyes saw my unformed body.
All the days ordained for me were written
in your book before one of them came to be."

[PSALM 139:13-16 NIV]

God's Word has held true in my life. It is essential because it is a constant reminder of His love for me. His protection has surrounded me from the day of my conception through every step of my life.

These personal stories and several miracle stories help to explain how God is as "real" to me as the person sitting next to me.

Carried by Faith

It began on a hot, humid August day in 1996. My husband on his 1993 Dyna Wide Glide Harley, our good friends on their Harley Davidson 1990 883 Sportster, and I on my 1992 1200 Sportster Harley rode down Interstate 90 between Rapid City and Sturgis, South Dakota to the Sturgis Bike Rally. It was our friends' inaugural ride into Sturgis during Bike Week. The sheer number of motorcycles gathered in one place was indescribable. As the saying goes, "If I must explain it, you would never understand." Our friends were beyond excited to witness this event for the first time.

Semis, cars, RV's, and motorcycles pushed along the Interstate. The seventy-five-mph speed limit made for fast and furious traveling. Numerous vehicles were weaving in and out of traffic, passing "slower" cars. Others, like us, stayed in the lane, taking it all in while focusing on the contour of the road.

The temperature hovered close to 100 degrees. Before leaving Rapid City for the twenty-six-mile ride to Sturgis, I took off my helmet and leather jacket to try to stay cool. I snuggly strapped them on top of my canvas bag with bungee cords on the back side of my Harley. I did not want them slipping out so I secured them, checking to make sure they would not be going anywhere. The hot breeze felt cool on my bare arms since I was wearing just a tank top and vest. But, that was the only part of me that was cool because I wore jeans and riding boots.

We cruised along in staggered format as is customary while riding in a motorcycle group. We kept a comfortable distance behind an RV, with my husband in the lead. I rode in the second position, while our friends were in the third position. Behind them, there were several other motorcycles, a common sight during Bike Week.

As my husband led our group, I could tell he was getting anxious and wanted to increase our pace. Sometimes I did not like his decisions on when to pass or move as a group. On this day, he pulled into the passing lane, blowing by the RV ahead of us. I had to follow because it is too easy to lose one another in this kind of traffic. Keeping in a staggered arrangement, I positioned myself to pass the RV. Our friends took my vacated spot, and we both made ready to pass to keep up with my husband. I scanned my surroundings, keeping vigilant of the fast-moving vehicles to my left and right. I was now the leader of the group. Preparing to pass the RV, I blinked. My life forever changed.

Without warning, my motorcycle began jerking from side to side as well as back and forth. Time seemed to slow as I realized a disaster was about to take place. I had lost control of my motorcycle while speeding at seventy plus miles per hour. I felt hopeless, and I knew my life was coming to a quick and painful end. It sounds cliché, but it is true: my life passed before my eyes. *My deepest thoughts were of my husband, my young son, and my soon-ending life!*

The Story of My Life Begins

I was the first child of two very opposite types of individuals who met during a hospital stay. He was a patient, and she was his nurse. My dad aspired to be in the business world. He grew up on a small farm. Farming was a family affair, and he was taught how to work hard from a very young age. Once he graduated from high school, he left for college. A few years later, he graduated with a four-year degree in business management.

My mom was from a rural area just outside a large city. After she graduated high school, she aspired to become a nurse. She entered nursing school at the small community college close to the farm where my dad grew up. Having met on a blind date, she would later serve as his nurse while he was in the hospital. My father won my mom's heart with his carefree attitude and love for fun. She could not resist. Shortly after meeting they were married.

Being young, adventurous, and wanting to be in the business world, they decided to leave the farm. Their first adventure took them to a metropolitan area to try big-city living and his hand in the business community. After a few years of the hustle and bustle of city life, they returned to the farm to continue the family farming tradition and to raise a family.

Discovery Years

 This is what I
REMEMBER
from this time
IN MY LIFE...

Daddy's Girl

Daddy's girl, the apple of my daddy's eye. I felt very special because I was the first born and he gave me a lot of attention. He would take me everywhere he went. He showed me off to friends, hugged me, and would do special things with me.

Just a little over two years later my brother arrived. He would grow up to be the one who took over the family farm. Then, six years later my youngest brother came along as the last of the three siblings in our family. My baby brother was born in the middle of harvest season. Eight years older than he was, I was very excited to be a big sister.

With three children and a farming business to operate, the special place I held in my daddy's eye seemed to dim. His focus on life was *not* me anymore. Being successful at farming and making a financially sound living took my place.

Fairy Tale Dreams

When I was around six years old, I imagined, my life would turn out a certain way. The dreams came alive while I was playing in my favorite place — my playhouse. It was one-story, one-room playhouse with a door and a single window, located in the backyard at our farm. I created pictures in my mind of my future with a handsome husband, children, and living in a two-story house.

As I played, the dreams evolved; my husband was handsome with lots of muscles and had nice wavy, light brown hair. He always paid attention to me and gave me lots of compliments. He made me feel safe and secure by taking good care of me financially, and he kissed me to show me how much he loved me.

The two-story house was a beautiful light yellow with white trim. It was big and had lots of rooms; several bedrooms, a nice sized family room, a formal dining room, and a huge kitchen. It even had a finished basement for the children to have a big play area.

Our children, only a few, were all well behaved and when they were not inside playing they were running and playing in the well-groomed yard. Lovely red rose bushes and a white picket fence trimmed the yard.

I continually had those dreams; at the time, my innocent young mind would not have been able to come up with the many interesting adventures and close calls that were in front of me.

Dreams of a young girl whose life was just getting started — would the fairy-tale ever come true?

Farm Life

Growing up on the farm I learned to love many things in the wide-open space of nature; like the smell of dirt, a barn's aroma, fresh cut hay, and harvest during the heat of summer. Also, I loved the simple things like taking drives to look at how the crops were progressing and gazing at the beautiful colors displayed at sunset. Of course, there was always an adventure or should I say, mischief to be had on the farm.

Hard work was the biggest trait instilled in me from being raised on a farm. We all worked hard and accom-

plished many things. When everyone pitched in, the job got done a lot faster. Regardless of your age or size, your help was always needed.

My parents depended on me to help take care of the house, cook, and help with my brothers, along with doing some outside chores. I was very responsible and loved to do all I could to help and get my parents' approval, especially my dad's. The main reason they needed my help was that my mom was dad's hired hand and she needed to start working early in the morning at the same time dad started. He was doing what he was taught, utilizing all the family members to have a good farming business. Plus, if ethnicity came into play — he simply was taught by his Russian German parents to start your day early and work hard all day! It was farm life.

Red Rubber Boots

My trait of never being idle and constantly thinking up something to keep me busy goes back to when I was very young. I remember one rainy spring day I was inside on the couch with my chin perched in my hands looking out the window watching the rain create a mud puddle in our front yard. It only arrived after it rained and would quickly disappear as soon as the sun would break through the clouds and with its heat bake the ground to absorb the water to make it hard, dry crackled clay.

The puddle was like candy sitting on a table in which mom would say, "Do not touch." I had been in the house too long waiting for the rain to stop. Sitting still was not easy for a busy-minded girl. A thought came to me, *"My red rubber boots!"* I loved those boots, which I so infrequently got to wear. I decided the mud puddle and the red rubber boots needed to meet each other. My boring, afternoon became one of an exciting adventure.

Those boots were in excellent condition since I did not get to wear them much. I liked them; they were such a pretty shade of red, my favorite color, still shiny, and not too scuffed up. Retrieving them from the closet, I would be extra careful in trying not to get them too dirty. My mom taught me that if you wanted to make sure not to get your socks dirty or wet, use extra protection by wearing plastic bread bags inside the boots like a second pair of socks. I decided this would be a good idea. I found two bags and put them over my white socks before sliding on my boots. Now, I felt confident, and I was ready to go outside.

Off I tromped to take advantage of the short-lived mud puddle. Entering on the edge and slowly stepping one foot in front of the other, I was focusing on my goal. It was simple, to reach the center of the puddle and see how deep it was.

Inching ever so close to the center there were only a few more steps to go, and my goal would be met. Each step I took became increasingly difficult as the mud began to feel like a suction cup and it did not want to release my boots. The few remaining steps were hard work on my legs with the muscles being strained every time I pulled my leg up to take another step.

Success! I arrived in the center. It is hard to stay stable in the thick, murky muck. The depth was up to the top of my boots which were now looking more like a perfect shade of ashy brown. With my goal met, retreating to the edge would be easy, or so I thought.

The mud felt like quick-drying cement, and it did not want to release me to lift my foot to make the first exit step. I stood still as I was thinking, *"How will I get out of this escapade without being caught?"*

The red rubber boots would have to stay put in the center of the puddle because I could not get them out. I would use my backup plan, the plastic bread bags, to make it to the edge. But, they were too thin and flimsy to stand up to the thick mud. Within a few feeble steps, they also succumbed to the mud. I would reach the dry ground in my now brown socks.

There was no way to hide from this mess. It was extremely noticeable from a trail left behind me of dirty pants, filthy socks, and muddy footprints. In addition to the bread bags that were nearly overtaken by mud and my stranded boots in the middle looking like a bullseye on a target. My goal was met!

Those boots remained in the center of the mud puddle until the hot sun dried the puddle. Once this happened, then it was easy to retrieve them, simply walk to the center on the visibly dry cracked dirt to yank at them a few times and out they came. Those red rubber boots were never quite the same, more like dull brown boots.

The moral of the story — sitting idle will never bring adventure.

Gas and Diesel Do Not Mix

A typical day on the farm would be full of busyness. We all would pitch in with the many things to do: taking care of farm equipment, moving vehicles to different fields, cleaning out grain bins, mowing grass, fencing, and feeding animals. My brother and I would help with some of these chores, and when we were done, we would roam around until another adventure captured our attention.

One day my brother decided to keep busy by sitting on top of a free-standing diesel tank located next to a bulk tank of regular gasoline. No harm. I noticed he had a large plastic drinking cup with him and the nozzle from the regular gasoline tank in his hands. He proceeded to fill the plastic cup with regular gasoline and then pour it into the diesel tank. I noticed him repeatedly doing this and knew it was not a good idea. My immediate reaction was to find dad and tell him. I decided to watch the situation unfold before my eyes to gather as much information as I could before finding dad. I knew he would get in big trouble.

After many cups of regular gasoline were dumped into the diesel tank, my evidence was collected, and I finally went to tell dad. He was angry with both of us, not just my brother like I had thought. He was mad at my brother for mixing the fuels and me for not coming to tell him sooner. For many years, the tank of blended fuels sat unused. It was not good for much more than using in a lawnmower.

The moral of the story — tell the truth and tell it quickly.

Clouds, Grass, and Max

My love for the outdoors sits deep in my soul. As young as I can remember, my favorite place to be was outside. The fresh smells and sights and sounds would capture my senses.

A favorite pastime on a beautiful summer day would be to find a perfect spot on the grass in our front yard and lay on my back to watch clouds. Big, fluffy, white cotton ball clouds in the brightest blue summer sky. My partner, Max, a Husky-German Shepard mix dog would position himself close to me. I loved Max because he always was by my side regardless of the type of adventure I would be on. He never judged me and always was happy to spend time with me.

I frequently enjoyed this activity. Each time I would position myself in just the right spot on the fresh smelling grass so any buildings would not block my view. While lying there in the grass, I would look up toward the vast open sky painted in the prettiest blue and gaze at the pure white clouds. Amazed at how big, fluffy, and puffy some of the clouds became as they rolled in the sky. For the longest time, I would let my imagination go wild on what I could see in each cloud. The clouds would form pictures in my mind of every imaginable object possible, but mostly animals; elephants, giraffes, dinosaurs, rabbits, clown faces, or a turtle.

I would lie there and enjoy the smell of the fresh summer breeze and how its gentle touch on my face felt. Just like feeling the tickling and prickling of the grass on my back. I delighted in how freeing it made me and how it released all the surrounding circumstances. It was a freedom of being totally lost in the openness of the sky.

The moral of the story — be still and enjoy nature.

Dolls and Playhouse

Another favorite pastime of mine was playing with dolls. I had several types of dolls; baby dolls, fashion dolls, and Barbie dolls. My doll collection consisted of the traditional baby dolls with opening and closing eyes — some even made crying noises — fashion dolls with hair pieces and pierced ears, and Barbie and Ken dolls.

My mom was an excellent seamstress and would sew doll clothes for many types of dolls, especially Barbie clothes. I remember watching her sew those small pieces together, thinking, *"I don't think I could ever sew those small pieces together."* My dolls were the best dressed, and each had an extensive wardrobe. For hours, I could be kept busy changing their clothes. All their clothes were stored in my playhouse, one of my favorite places to be. The dolls would be my imaginary friends, and I believed they loved the playhouse just as much as I did.

The one-story, one room playhouse had a door and one window and was painted white inside and out. It was filled with so many fun things to keep me busy all day long; a pretend stove, pots, and pans, dress up clothes, furniture, and my dolls. The playhouse sat in the backyard behind our house near a big tree.

The tree had two swings strategically placed on one massive limb. One swing was a tire swing, and the other had a rope with a wooden seat nestled in it to make it the faster of the two. When I tired of the playhouse, I would play on the swings.

The pretend kitchen was stocked with pots and pans to make all kinds of great recipes. I made fantastic cuisine using mostly play dough; little berries for pies with lattice crust top, cinnamon rolls carefully constructed with two colors of play dough. As I made all these exotic dishes, my dolls would sit quietly in their chairs watching me bake and waiting for a special treat.

I thought my playhouse was the absolute best until I was invited to a friend's house to play. Her playhouse was bigger and nicer. A two-story house with several rooms on the main floor. It was nicely furnished with a stove, fridge, table, chairs, and other items to make it a fun place to pretend. After visiting my friend's playhouse, playing in my house seemed less satisfying. Nonetheless, my playhouse was a place I wanted to go every day.

It was lonely playing by myself, and I always wanted others to play with me. My brother was off doing some other boy thing, and mom would come out occasionally to play. My dream was to have another girl my age to play with all day long. Instead, I would play by myself and day-dream about how it would be when I was all grown up and had a family of my own and a big beautiful house with a white picket fence.

The moral of the story — dare to dream.

Driving Lesson

Being raised on a farm, we had access to a wide-open territory to play as kids. As we grew older and became more responsible for chores and duties around the farm, we were taught how to drive. We were still quite young.

The first vehicle I learned to drive was a 1968 Dodge station wagon, which dad bought at an auction. He always found good deals on many types of vehicles. The day he brought this one home he came cruising into our farmyard saying, "I could not let this deal pass me. I got it for $200. It was a steal of a deal." It was a nice sky-blue color with a wood panel in the center section of the exterior. The interior was also sky blue, and it had a rumble seat in the very back.

Dad expected us to learn quickly with very little instruction given to most anything he would teach us to do, and this would be no different. Luckily, I was a fast learner and eager to please him. Here is how I remember the driving lesson. Dad was in the passenger seat; being only eight years old I was sitting right on the edge of the driver's seat grabbing onto the huge steering wheel to keep myself close enough to reach the floorboard and the pedals. I was ready for the instructions to begin. Dad pointed at the gearshift attached to the steering column and said, "See this, take it and pull down until the pointer goes in front of the letter D, then press on this floor pedal to make it go. When you want to stop, press on the pedal next to the one that makes it go." That was the end of instructions! Now I was ready to try it. I did as he said and as we began to be shifted back and forth, dad said, "I think you are getting the hang of it." I was now an official driver.

Why do you teach your kids to drive at a such a young age? Of course, to help on the farm! I would help move vehicles from field to field and drive the tractor to do field-work. This was normal for most farm kids that I knew.

Having the imaginative mind, I would always think of something else to do with this newly learned skill. When my brother and I were left alone on the farm, we usually found mischief. During one of these times, we decided to have a little fun in that 1968 Dodge.

I was the driver, and my brother was the passenger. I would keep my eyes closed, and he would instruct me to drive by telling me where to go around the yard. He would be perched in the passenger seat yelling, "Go left, right, straight, stop!" It was a fun game. We never hit anything, but I know we came close. The biggest thing was we never got caught by our parents.

The moral of the story — never leave two very creative-thinking children by themselves for too long.

The End of Dolls and Playhouse

Those play times of pretending with dolls and dishes in my playhouse turned into real-life occurrences. When I was eight years old, my youngest brother was born. Being the only daughter, my parents felt I could help take care of my new baby brother. My mother depended on me to help with both of my brothers and the house at this young age.

Mom and dad were busy trying their hardest to make a living. With my mom working alongside my father as a hired hand; having me take care of my younger brothers, it would be helpful and less expensive than hiring a babysitter to watch all of us while they worked the farm.

Mom knew she could rely on me to do what she asked. I was responsible at this young age. However, I did not want to take care of my brothers. I did not think I would like babysitting like other girls. I wanted to play outside where

19

there were so many more liberties. But, that was not what my parents had in mind.

They had convinced me. I could do it! Watch my brothers, make a simple meal, hang the laundry out to dry on the clothesline, and play outside to keep busy. It seemed okay, especially when they said if I needed anything all I had to do was call them on the CB radio. I liked talking on the CB radio, and I felt this would be okay. They were usually close to the farmyard anyway. So, I thought I would help.

Most of the time, watching my brothers was all right. My brother closest to me in age was usually off doing something mischievous. My baby brother was like a doll, except he wiggled and cried way too much. I did learn how to change diapers, clothe and feed him but all of it became very real, and it was NOT like playing pretend with my dolls.

There were some scary, fearful times taking care of my younger brothers. Many times, I did not know what to do with this baby. He would cry so hard, and no matter what I tried he would not stop crying. Sometimes when he cried, he would lose his breath. I would blow in his face to help give him some oxygen and then he would gasp and start wailing again. I thought he was going to die.

I wanted to please my parents and have them tell me how proud they were of me, what a good job I was doing, and how much they loved me, particularly my dad. I tried hard at all the things I was supposed to do. Still, it seemed whatever compliment they gave me, it was never enough; I always wanted more.

After a few years of taking care of my brothers, I became angry about this responsibility. Anger was becoming a familiar friend inside me as a response to many things; it was a feeling I understood, and it was always at the surface of my emotions.

When I did have time away from the responsibilities my parents gave me, I would play with my dolls in my playhouse. I realized that it was not as much fun playing make believe anymore because I was doing all these things in real life. The real world was in my life to stay.

This realism reignited my anger. All the dolls I cherished so much, I took them and opened my closet door to throw all of them along with their beautifully sewn clothes into the farthest end of my closet. I would no longer be playing with pretend dolls and their beautifully sewn clothes in my fun playhouse. No, I would have a live baby and brother to take care of in a live house. Real life had hit me hard. As I grew older, the playhouse and I grew further apart. Eventually, the playhouse turned into a storage shed.

The moral of the story — imaginative play is important for young children.

Christmas Memory

I remember an exceptional Christmas program at our little community church. A mother of a classmate who was creative and loved to work with children directed the Christmas program that year. She was such a fun and loving woman who not only helped at church but also at school where she gave guitar and vocal lessons.

The program was anything but ordinary. Not the run of the mill, typical, stand in front of the congregation and quote a few verses and sing a few songs, Christmas program. No, it would be one with lasting memories for many. Several Sundays before the program we practiced our parts and worked on costumes. We even had a few additional practices to make sure we were ready for what would be an extraordinary program.

The special Sunday had finally arrived, our costumes were ready, lines twirling in our minds, and excitement was in the air. When we arrived at church everyone was excited to see what we had been working on for weeks. Everyone was told to keep their coats, hats, and mittens on and proceed to load onto a yellow school bus. The entire congregation was taken to a farm that was close by for our live production.

The scene was set in the barn; fresh rolled-out hay, cows mooing, horses instead of donkeys, sheep baaing, and a real baby for Jesus. Each of us kids quickly took our prepared costume fit to go over our warm coats, and we were ready to start reciting our well-memorized lines. It was the well-known, traditional story of the birth of Jesus in a manger. It became special because it was being told in the live scenery of the barn.

The program was short because it was cold outside. Everyone got back on the bus and returned to the church for hot cocoa, coffee, and treats. The pastor shared a few more things about the meaning of Christmas while all of us kids sat in the front row staring at the beautifully lit real Christmas tree. At the end of the service, all the children received a gift of a brown paper bag filled with shelled peanuts, chocolate, and hard candies and an apple. It was such a perfect way to end our time together.

The moral of the story — Christmas through the eyes of a child is never dull.

REFLECTION PAUSE

This time of my life was full of many carefree days. I loved nature and was free in it. There were no limitations outside, unlike the four walls of our house that felt confining. When I opened the front door, and stepped outside new life blew my way as I felt the fresh air blow in my face. I felt freedom most days and always would use my imagination. I was a very busy girl with an active mind, and hard to keep out of mischief.

My family was present and available, and I felt loved. I would seek out a lot of attention and words of affirmation. I was always looking for my parents' approval, especially from my father. Dad and mom seemed very busy and not able to spend as much time as I seemed to need. I wanted to be loved more and to be told I was good at the things I was doing.

Becoming responsible at a young age had the negative effect instilling fear in me, especially when it came to taking care of babies. I would rarely offer to babysit anyone else's children; it was too scary. I believe it was what sabotaged my desire to want to become a mother in the years to come. I swore I would never have children.

I did not know much about God or Jesus from my family life. I heard about Him as a cutout cartoon character hanging on a felt flannel board in Sunday School classroom. He was one of the characters in the many stories that were taught.

And the baby Jesus was the focus at Christmas time which did not make sense to me, how could a baby help me? The rest of Christmas was about pretty, sparkly trees, fancy decorations, and big presents. Other than that, I had no understanding or concept of who or what God did. He was not real to me. I did not know much about Him except He was talked about during Christmas and Easter.

Wondering Years

 This is what I
REMEMBER
from this time
IN MY LIFE...

Dirt Bike

Compared to learning how to drive a vehicle, finding out how to operate a motorcycle was easy and fun. Dad bought my brother and I a Kawasaki 80cc dirt bike when I was around the age of twelve and my brother was ten years old. I loved the freedom of riding a motorcycle — the wind in my hair, the different smells of the outdoors, and the sense of excitement at getting away from the farm. Our parents set limits on how far we could go from the farm. The boundary was one mile each way from the farm on the gravel road. We could go farther if it were on the prairie trails amongst our fields. After the hundredth time in one day of riding back and forth on the gravel road, we would inch past the mile border and eventually get to the highway which was two miles away.

We were supposed to share and divide up our time evenly driving this fun toy. The sharing of equal time always started out good, but, eventually, it would end badly. One time, I decided to take a longer ride when I got my turn. I would taunt and tease my brother each time I drove past him. This would infuriate him, and he finally had had enough. The next time I drove by him, he began to chase after me and got close enough to grab onto my waist. He refused to let go. Eventually, after his weight and wiggling around got to be too much, we both came crashing down. He wrestled me off the dirt bike and sped off to have a very long turn for himself. I never could underestimate the strong-willed nature of my brother.

Saturday Night Roller Skating

The most memorable activity of my preteen years was Saturday night roller skating; it was the highlight of the entire week. I looked forward to it because if we had not gotten off the farm all week, at least we knew we would on Saturday. My brother and I were determined to go each Saturday. Early each Saturday, I would pick out the outfit I would wear. One of my favorites was a pair of denim hip hugger jeans that were patterned with white and yellow checkers that I wore with a white belt. I would match it with a golden yellow t-shirt and finished it off by wearing a royal blue blouse tied at the waist. I would take a bath to make sure my long brown hair was nice and shiny, and it helped my oily skin where pimples were starting, especially on my forehead. However, my straight bangs would cover up most of them.

Every Saturday we would get a ride from dad to town. He would give us a few dollars to rent our skates, buy a pop and candy. It was fun to meet up with all my friends from school. We would skate for a while and then stop to huddle up and talk about what boys we liked. Mostly it was a time to practice skating and see how fast we could go, especially playing the skating games like Limbo.

As I got older, I noticed some kids would leave the roller rink for a while and then come back at the very end of the session when their parents picked them up. One time, my curiosity got the best of me, and I followed them to see what they were doing. They went to the picnic shelter in the city park and were smoking cigarettes and retrieving beer they had stashed in the bushes behind the shelter. I watched for a while and then one of them saw me and said, "Hey what are you doing?" I replied, "Nothing. Just wondering what you guys were doing." To make sure I kept quiet they invited me over and instructed me not to tell anyone. This was my first exposure to smoking and drinking. I was curious about them, so I wanted to stick around and find out more.

During one of those breaks from skating several of us went to the shelter at the park. My best friend's older cousin, who looked so grownup and cool, had come to visit, and she would show us how to smoke cigarettes. After several tries, lots of coughing, and our eyes burning from the smoke in our faces, we eventually got the hang of how to inhale. We felt cool and grown up just like her.

This was the beginning of a bad habit that lasted well into my twenties. Since my best friend and I started smoking and inhaling at such a young age, we had to keep the habit maintained. We began stealing cigarettes from her mom and dad and had it down to a science. My friend would make sure to lift one pack during the school week and then we would take another on Saturday. I never actually paid for cigarettes until I was in junior high when I could buy them for fifty cents out of a machine at the bowling alley.

The other bad habit, which started weekly on Saturday night roller skating, was experimenting with drinking alcohol. It started with wine and then beer. The only other time I had tasted alcohol was when I tried my dad's beer when I was approximately eight years old. I liked the bubbles and the way it made me feel dizzy, once I got past the stinky smell and the pain in my throat. It made me feel all warm inside.

It was easy for us to get wine. It tasted like juice to me and was easy for me to drink. The only thing I did not care for was the huge amount I had to drink to get the dizzy feeling I had felt with the beer. I loved how I felt when I drank alcohol, it made me feel light-headed, free of worries, and gave me courage like I never had before. I became brave, more talkative, prettier, and fearless. It filled the lonely hole in me like no person could fill, and it made me feel more accepted by others.

I felt like I belonged in the group when I drank. I was not okay with being by myself and did not feel like I fit in. But, when I drank it helped fill part of the black hole I felt in my soul. I was starving for attention. I would do whatever needed to be done to fit in.

Alcohol made me feel at ease, relaxed, and it numbed the many things from my home life. It was all I needed; it fixed everything. And so, the enticing dance with alcohol and cigarettes began.

My New Feeling Friends

By the age of twelve, my desire to distance myself from my parents and to be independent started. I would continually try to put physical space between us. There was an overwhelming feeling in me that I did not understand, but I did not want to be around them anymore. This is when the selfish, preteen thinking, *"It is all about me,"* started. Anger developed over what I felt was injustice from the responsibilities I was asked to do. My friends became increasingly important. All I saw were the differences with my parents more than the similarities. The foundation of my protective walls was being created.

As a family, most of our activities focused around working on the farm, and my parents seemed so preoccupied with the farm work and had little time to give me attention. I felt their work was the most important thing to them. The love and affection I so desired did not get filled at home, so I sought it from friends and school. This started around the same time as did the experimenting with smoking and drinking.

I would get very angry that my parents did not want to spend time with me; a catch twenty-two. I was the one who did not want to be around them. I was so confused in my mind. I wanted someone to talk to, to listen to me, and to express interest in me. It seemed to me, without an explanation from them, that they simply wanted me to work for them; free labor with no benefits and no relationship. This way of thinking made me more withdrawn from them and angrier.

Once the anger settled in my soul, it was like a smoldering fire just waiting for another log of injustice to be thrown on the fire to ignite the rage. To a preteen, the unfairness is irrational. In my forming mind, I began to despise the farm, my dad, and the work he made us do.

Anger became my go-to-friend in response to anything to do with my parents. I would constantly talk about how unjust it was to work so hard and have so many responsibilities at such a young age. I viewed these years as all work and a lot of yelling and little fun. Thus, anger became my comfort friend.

My friend, anger, continually convinced me of this while picking rocks in the field, hauling water out to a cow that had collapsed, shoveling grain, mowing the lawn, or doing chores. I began to realize how valuable my work was to them and that it could be used to my advantage. This was when anger introduced me to a new friend — manipulation — my new BFF (Best Friend Forever)!

My friend anger had such outbursts and at times was too volatile, so manipulation would calm things down to turn my devious thoughts to a calmer state of mind. When I could control myself and my thoughts I realized this was like a game, the "control game," and I wanted to *win*!

I wanted to win at the game of control so manipulation introduced me to lying. This companion showed me how to twist ideas to get my ultimate result. All these "feeling" friends would be used together to help me *win*. I thrived on it.

I began to scheme about ways to work things to my favor with my parents. If they wanted me to do something, then my "feeling friends" would discuss what they could get out of the deal, thinking, *"What was in it for me?"* Some of the ideas I had were not always good for me, yet I was "in control," or so I thought.

Control Game Gone Bad

Manipulation and control led me to some unsafe and harmful experiences. It started by thinking it would be fun to have a friend over who could help me babysit my younger brothers because it was lonely on the farm. Together we would do a better job watching and keeping them busy. I wanted nothing more than to hang out with my friend. My mom gave into my pleading and rationalizing that my friend, a year older, would help me babysit my brothers.

On one of the days we were babysitting, she was talking on the phone to some guys who were much older. They were in their twenties and from a bigger town nearby. I was listening as she said, "It was okay to come over to hang out." I did not think this was a good idea, but, what could I do? I could not tell my parents. I was in too deep because I was the one who wanted to have her help me.

The older guys were only interested in one thing, to take advantage of young, naïve girls. I thought the guy liked me and that maybe we could talk over the phone and hang out again but that was not the case. This rejection would be a wound etched deep in my soul, leaving a lifelong scar of damage. An innocent girl's view of love turned to ugly forces of ravish. My innocence quickly vanished, and shame and its heaviness began to hover over me.

This is when two habits started and lasted for many years. One of them was that I would stand in the shower with the hottest water my skin could handle to try to wash all the filth off me. I was hoping the sound of the shower would help drown out the painful cries I made and wash them down the drain. Stepping out of the shower, I would feel much better and know the filth was washed away, but there was no way I would ever look in the mirror at myself because I felt like dirty trash, thrown away. I believed I was so ugly that no one else would want to look at me. I blamed myself because I was the one who manipulated the situation and was in the wrong place at the wrong time. This was when the second habit began of never looking at myself eye to eye in the mirror. The shame was evident, and I felt it all around me. It felt like it radiated out of me. There was no way I could look myself in the eye to see the dirty trash I had become. Mirror, mirror on the wall, I will never look at myself at all.

Manipulation and Hateful Words

There was a time when my anger got out of control, and I was acting like a toddler in a preteen body having temper tantrums with screaming fits. I screamed so much to try to get my way I lost my voice several times. Mom sought out professional help, and I attended sessions with a speech therapist to learn how to use my voice box correctly. I was uncomfortable in my skin, not knowing how to handle touchy family situations and it did not help that my hormones were out of control. My parents did not have a clue what to do with me; mom had a quieter approach and dad was loud and angry. Everything seemed to be crumbling down around me.

I did not know what I wanted. In my world, my life was all about *me*, and nothing about anyone else. I was very self-focused. My view of life through my eyeglasses was skewed.

This self-centered view created constant tension between my parents and me. It was like a war. I was on one side, and they were on the other with no middle ground. I viewed them as the enemy. This created a hostile environment at times that escalated to a few incidents of explosions. I decided to take advantage of the situation and revealed information to other adult authorities in which social services were called in.

The threat of social services was the ammunition I needed to keep myself isolated and protected from conflict situations with my parents. Any time a spark of anger was thrown my way I would threaten to contact the authorities. This nasty battle started the hard reality of me using my go-to weapon of manipulation. It also began the difficult realism of physically separating myself from my parents, the walls of self-protection were continuing to be built.

These walls I built would not let my parents touch me. Mom was very affectionate and always gave lots of hugs. I did not like these and pushed her away or stood stone cold like a statue whenever she attempted to hug me. Dad was not a touchy-feely type of person and did not hug much anyway. After my constant threats and ice-cold barriers were created, he never did hug me again. Any physical contact I once received in love from him was now gone. It was easier for him to not engage in any physical contact. The person I loved so much and tried so hard to please would now distance himself from me.

Whatever love was there between father and daughter dwindled ever so slowly. As the years of no communication, lack of trust, and no interest in my activities in my life became more frequent, the relationship dwindled fast. He replaced physical contact with hurtful words that turned to burning arrows into my heart. Hate was birthed in my heart for this man who I once cherished and loved so much. What he said about me embedded in my mind and twisted my perception of myself. I would give him something to talk about and thought, *"If he thinks I'm so bad, then I will show him how bad."*

The verbal slashing beat my already broken spirit; the words stung like a freshly exposed wound to the air. The sting would take my breath away. For me to protect myself and not let the words tear me down, I would show no emotion and no tears. I hated my dad for what he said about me. Mentally trying to handle the descriptive words tumbling around in my mind was exhausting. There was no controlling my thoughts; they were like untamed wild horses. The problem was that I would not share these thoughts with anyone and the toll was starting to wear me down. I needed someone to confide in so I would have some relief from these ideas. I decided to let a few new friends into my walls of protection to surround me — they were Mr. Alcohol and Mrs. Drug. They did not speak any audible hurtful words about me. They were comforting, soothing, and made everything disappear and specialized in numbing my mind from raging thoughts. My new friends calmed me down and tamed my wild mind.

I invited these friends into my life because I did not know how to cope with my emotions. I sought out whatever could numb me and alcohol, and drugs were my choice. Drugs and alcohol were easy for me to get because I was hanging out with much older people.

Alcohol and drugs numbed me from reality. It shut down my crazy thoughts and quieted all the negative words circling in my mind and made me feel relaxed. They gave me courage, energy, and beauty. I never wanted to end my relationship with these "friends." Many times, I would go on benders with them for several days, always wanting more and more time with them.

This craziness was dragging me deeper into the depths of Hell. The dark feelings were so intense, so close, and so deep inside of me I felt like I could touch Hell. Isolating. Empty. Torturing. Never-ending.

Mom's Idea of Help

During this time of beginning a new friendship with alcohol and drugs, my mom was desperately trying to help me. Of course, I was on a fast-spinning free fall to the pit of Hell. She was seeking help from wherever she could find it. She asked women at the Christian Women's Club at church to please pray for her daughter who was lost and needed to find God. She also would try and share with me about God and one time she gave me a Bible. I pushed it away. I did keep it, and after she was gone I flipped through a few pages, but the words made no sense. All I heard were negative words, "Look who you are hanging out with. God's going to get you. You are going to Hell if you keep hanging out with those friends and doing those things." It felt so condemning and hopeless.

My dear mom so terribly wanted to help me in any way she could. In her quest to find help, she felt enrolling me in confirmation class at church may help. She may have thought it would stop my bad behaviors of hanging out with wrong kids, drinking, smoking, and doing drugs. I begrudgingly agreed to the idea and went to the class. It was an awkward place to be with kids I did not hang out with or have anything in common. When I was there, I felt like a science experiment, what will happen if we say this to her or what reaction will we get if this is mentioned? The environment was not warm and friendly but it was partially my fault because my walls of protection were so high and strongly built.

One time the pastor was reminding the group about needing to memorize all the books of the Bible and the Ten Commandments as part of the requirement to be confirmed. *"What?"* Memorizing something I knew nothing about was going to be impossible, not to mention it was one thing I hated the most. *"How was this going to be any fun?"* I decided I would try it. I went home and attempted to memorize, but it was extremely difficult. There was too much to remember, and I was not one bit interested. I could not understand the rationale behind it. My big question was, *"Why?"*

After my feeble attempt to memorize the Books of the Bible and the Ten Commandments I decided to challenge the pastor and asked, "Why do we have to memorize all this stuff anyway?" His response was one stamped into my memory forever; it is like he spoke it yesterday. He said, "If you do not memorize them, you will go to Hell!" Well, that was it, it was the fuel needed to be poured on the hot, smoldering ember in my soul. The soul that was looking for any reason to say, *"I told you this God thing is a hoax."*

Once this fiery statement of reality shot through a small crack in my wall, it put an inferno of flames in me to justify every reason to tell him exactly what I thought. My response is one I also will never forget. I replied in a cold, calculated, matter of fact tone, "If that is the case then I am in HELL!" These piercing words struck back at him, he called my mom to inform her of our conversation and said, "I was not welcome at the class anymore."

After this event, my new goal was to act like the words people were using to describe me, mischievous and rebellious, did not hurt me. Hiding behind my protective walls was much easier to do than dealing with people.

Protective Walls Built

The protective walls I built started out low and were a self-protection mechanism. They became comfortable for me to hide behind because no one bugged me with their emotions, their affections, or their need to care for me. I blocked out most people; it was easier than letting them in and getting hurt. I knew one thing for sure; no one was getting through these walls.

In this isolating place I had built, there was plenty of time to think and ponder on all the things others said about me. My thoughts battled endlessly and tortured me daily when I allowed my mind to dwell on the words and accusations. The terrible things said of me began to grow in me and become part of me. Orneriness and anger are what came out of me; they were my protection from feeling any pain of the hurtful words. As I continued to push others away, my self-confidence slid into the gutter. I was not interested in letting anyone in the fortress of walls.

Brick by brick the walls continued to be built. I felt like no one understood me, so silence and anger was my response. Anger is the tag along of bitterness, and it would be a good friend for many years. Indifference was growing stronger in my heart toward my parents and others.

My desperate thoughts would lead me to seek out attention and affections in many wrong ways. Desperate people will do desperate things to be accepted. I thought the people I was hanging around were *"My friends. That they wanted to be with me. They liked me for who I was."* They seemed only to want "things," and not my friendship. I would even steal money from my parents so they would keep "liking" me. The harsh reality was these people were not true friends, and they were simply using me.

The continued heaviness of not feeling accepted by others was a frustrating reality for me, and it began to weigh me down. I kept trying to figure out people and why I was getting mistreated. I could not understand the part I played in it. I needed help from other adults that could explain what I was going through as a teenager. To help me understand and to find ways to deal with my feelings of inadequacy and not fitting in. I needed to share with another adult, but, I refused to ask for any help from my parents.

I would continue down this crazy path with no insight from others. All alone in my isolated world surrounded by rationalized self-built walls, thinking it was the best place for me to be. It was a dangerous place for a young teenager. It became a situation where trying to understand reality was too confusing. And so, the journey continued inside the dark, lonely walls.

Walls as a Way of Life

The high, thick walls of protection became my life; they bordered my heart so no one could enter. Others did not understand what I was living in, this *living Hell.* The walls hid the pain and unspeakable things associated with the hard years of alcohol and drug abuse. I believed no one would understand, so it was easier to keep everyone away with high, cold walls of silence and no emotion. No form of light, goodness, or happiness was allowed in. If there were a slight crack in the mortar, anger would fill in the crevasse so the light of life and goodness could never enter.

These walls were very real to me and neatly built in my mind. They were constructed like walls in an ancient city, which had two sets of walls erected with an area between them for storage, housing, or hiding. It was a protective barrier so if the enemy broke down one wall, the second one would continue to keep things out. This is how I viewed my emotional surroundings: you may get through one wall, but you would never get through the second wall, the one closest to my heart.

Alcohol and Drugs Filled the Silence

It was nice and quiet in the walls of protection, I did not have to explain myself, but then again, I could not explain myself. The silence was best, and that is why I would use the "liquid forgetter," alcohol and drugs. I craved the effect they gave me, and they kept my level of chaotic thinking at bay. It started to do for me what I could not do for myself. I ran after the effect and did whatever I needed to get my supply. The concoctions of alcohol and drugs along with the need to keep my supply met took me to some very dark places. It can be explained like this — wickedness danced in the darkness of night, moving in and out of its hiding places and drunkenness was the painful bondage that took over my mind and body. When I would awaken from its stupor, I would wonder, *"Where am I?" "What happened to me?" "What have I done?"*

Crying and trying to hide the tears so no one could see my face, I would ask myself, *"Who was this 'no one' lying next to me?"* I was lying in bed with dirty sheets and smells to make my stomach turn. I wanted to leave this filthy place, escaping was my only thought, *"I have to get out."*

"What was to become of my miserable life? Why was I here anyway?" I looked for a way to escape my life, even a slit to my wrist one dark night would not stop the pain. I had no answers. It felt like a knife stabbing in my heart. The pain would dull occasionally, but I always felt its continual throb, reminding me of my bondage.

I was a black-out drinker with a very high tolerance level. I would drink as much as I physically could hold in my stomach and when I needed more room I would make myself throw up. By adding some street drug to the mix, it would allow me to stay up for days at a time. I was constantly trying to get back to the original first feeling of catching a "buzz" or "getting high."

No Escape

Nights turned into weeks, then months and years of crying and sobbing into my pillow. My pillow stopped the loud wail coming from deep within my soul. It silenced the fear and absorbed the tears that I could not vocalize. No words would ever reach my lips to explain my hopelessness. I continued to repeat in my head, *"Why God ... why am I here?"* I did not have any answers, so I continued to hide behind my protective walls.

Hiding my tears and pain was like flipping a light switch on and off. One moment I would be bawling my eyes out and the next moment, drying my eyes with my pillowcase and using a cold washcloth compression to reduce the swelling of my red, puffy eyes so I could go out and be around others. My parents would ask, "Are you okay?" My silence continued because I was unable to describe my feelings.

My parents seemed distant and unapproachable; they had their own worries in life. My dad yelled a lot and was full of anger about things I did not understand. I loved him, and he seemed to love me, but that felt like years ago, when I was a little girl. Those memories were long gone and his attention just as far away.

Mom tried to keep everything together. With unspoken words, I instinctively knew there was conflict. The confusion and disagreement of how to parent a challenging kid was like a big elephant in the room, and you automatically knew it was the "major conflict." She did her best to balance the "us" and "them," kids and parents.

At times, I wanted to tell my parents I needed help, to ask them to pay attention to me, to hug me, and to spend more time with me. But, the walls were built too high, and I could not let them in. I deeply yearned to be told I was loved and that all these emotions were a part of growing up, and that everything would be okay. I did not know how to express myself and silence remained as I continued to bottle up all my thoughts.

Being loved and accepted by my parents and peers was an overbearing concern which never escaped my thoughts. I needed validation and assurance about the many questions that circled in my mind: "*Were these thoughts realistic and normal?*" Once again, silence ruled in my young mind with the lingering, desperate questions. I started to look for anything to help me feel love and acceptance. It felt like there was no direction in my life, no dreams, and no goals. My mind was frozen and entrapped in a cycle of empty hopelessness.

My parents and siblings were no longer as important as my friends. These "friends" were simply "trouble." My downfall was wanting attention and seeking it in the wrong places.

I had seen, heard, and done too many bad things. I went too far, far enough to see the eyes of evil and the intense darkness of Hell. Lured to dark places where illegal and immoral activities happened I could not escape the activities or the people. I was given the attention my mind was seeking. The search for someone, anyone to love me was found. Or so I thought.

The enemy took me places I should never have been, and with people I had no business being around. He wanted to take me down, flush me out, and destroy any hope of a future for my life. I felt unforgiven, marred with evil, and saturated with a heavy blanket of dark sin. This was a jail and Hell on earth. Freedom was only for the clean, pure, and untouched people. I believed there was too much darkness in me to be set free, cleaned up, or forgiven.

Fear did not exist in me; my emotions had left long ago. Emptiness and gut-wrenching pain were the only feelings I understood. The remedy to push everything down for temporary relief was more alcohol and drugs.

The girlish daydream of the white picket fence, trimmed yard and house were gone. They would not be allowed to enter my mind again because I knew how far down this bad path I had traveled. The hopes and dreams trickled away, and thoughts of how to survive in this dark world of lower levels of existence took over and became reality.

Consequences of Hiding in the Darkness

A deadly combination of drinking and driving became a habit for me. I only had my learner's permit, but I manipulated my parents into letting me drive by myself without the required licensed driver being with me. I loved to drive anywhere I could, especially "Hill Cruising" — what we called it where I grew up.

Late one night after driving a friend home I made my way down a residential side street trying to get through town and head home without being caught because I was driving alone. I had been drinking heavily that evening and frequently would black out. I tried my hardest to keep the car driving straight in the lane of the street but it was a challenge or so said the deputy following me; I nearly hit a parked car before he pulled me over.

This time I would have severe consequences. I was arrested for DUI (driving under the influence) at the age of fifteen years old. I was taken to the holding tank for juveniles at the county sheriff's department while my parents were called. The court postponed the case for twelve months with the following conditions — one, I was to refrain from the use of alcohol and have no driving or liquor violations during that time. Two, I could have no pleasure driving. Three, I was to be supervised by a probation officer monthly. Four, I was to have no association with people using alcohol. Five, I was not allowed to frequent places where alcohol was being served.

My name was put in the local paper with the other offenders, and I was expelled from all extracurricular activities I was involved in at school. This news created more people in the community talking about me. I began to believe the hurtful words from parents of kids I knew at school. Any classmates that were friends were now instructed by their parents to have no contact with me. This led me straight to the older friends who told me, "This is just a legal bump in the road and no big deal."

I hated everything about the conditions of my probation and particularly hated the probation officer. He was a meek, quiet, and an easy to run over man in his forties. Our personalities were very different and he, like any other adult in my life, was just another irritant and a challenge to see how quickly I could make him angry and manipulate him. Within six months, he'd had enough, and referred me for an alcohol evaluation in hopes of handing me off to another agency to finish the remaining time of my probation. As he stated in the letter to my parents, he expected me to cooperate in this program with honesty and openness.

The alcohol evaluation was in a city approximately one hundred miles away. I convinced my parents that I would drive myself to the classes. They agreed, so off I went with without the required licensed driver that was needed.

It was the first time I had spoken to anyone about my drinking, and I heard the term used to describe me — "borderline alcoholic." I did not know what this was, but I surely was not it. The new agency assigned me to attend alcohol education classes for several months; I called them "drunk classes." I do not remember much of anything from the classes. My focus every week was to go to a friend's house and party for an hour or two before driving the long trip home.

I still did not have an official driver's license. The law would however allow me to receive it even though I was arrested for a DUI. I just needed to pass the written test along with the behind the wheel driving portion and I would be a legal driver. The problem was that the local county sheriff's department made it clear that even though I legally could receive my driver's license they were the ones conducting the behind the wheel portion of the exam, and it would be very difficult to pass the test if it was up to them. I decided to go to the next county to take the test and get my license. Nothing would stop me; getting a DUI, probation, or an alcohol education class, nothing!

Friend, Black Out

My sidekick friend, Black Out, still wanted to hang out and seemed to be a constant companion. Several times when I was driving it would cozy up to me. I could sense it getting close then I would pull off the road, take the keys out of the ignition, lock the doors, and sleep for a few hours. I would awake several hours later, usually to bright sunshine in my eyes and look to see if the coast was clear so I could take off as if nothing had happened. One time, I was awakened by a loud knock on the driver's side window by the local county sheriff. He was saying, "Open the door and let's talk." NOT! There was no way I would open the locked doors, if I did, it would guarantee more trouble. *"How was I going to get out of this one?"* I refused to open the door, so he called my mom, who he knew. She came to where we were to try to convince me to cooperate. I eventually opened the door and let them take my keys. No charges were filed against me because I think the sheriff felt sorry for my mom, who was exhausted in having to deal with a daughter like me.

I was so self-centered and absorbed that not once did I think about how my parents felt during this fast-self-destructive mode I was in. All my mom would say to me is, "I am praying for you." What she said went in one ear and out the other, I did not care.

Every time I drank, which was three to four times a week, this sidekick was with me. I continued to drive under the influence of alcohol and drugs, it progressively getting worse. I continued to drink and drug on a weekly basis and never wanted to stop. This led me to find new ways to mix the right substance together to get the numbness and consciousness I was looking for to stay awake day and night. I never wanted the night to end.

Early one evening a friend dropped me off at home and it seemed much too early for the night to end. I wanted to keep partying and decided to see if another friend would join me. My car was low on gas, so I decided to take my dad's farm pickup without his permission. I would only be gone for a few hours and have it back in time for him to leave for the farm come sunrise.

This pickup was used to service and fuel the farm equipment and had dual gas tanks that would exchange gas from one to the other by a switch on the dashboard. In the pickup box, there were two bulk tanks, one with diesel and one with regular gas for fueling equipment.

To get the keys I quietly went into the house, reached quickly behind the front door to grab them and off I went. I proceeded to take a joy ride to this friend's house some ten miles away. I remember leaving our house and driving down the road. The next thing I recall is thinking, *"I need to take a shortcut down a prairie trail so I would not get caught driving drunk."* I turned down a dirt road and sidekick black out saddled up to me, and the next thing I remember is looking out the windshield at water.

I had driven into a big slough and was stuck in the middle with thick mud all around. I tried my hardest to get unstuck by going back and forth, but the weight of the two fuel tanks in the backend made it impossible to get out. I tried for so long that I ran one of the tanks out of gas, switched to the other dual tank to find it was empty. I had totally run out of gas. The slough had engulfed the pickup. *"Now what was I going to do?"* I opened the driver's side door and water began running inside. I quickly shut the door and determined the window would be my escape route. I climbed out onto the top of the diesel tank in the box of the pickup. After standing there surmising what I had gotten myself into, I had no other choice but to go get help. I wanted to try and fix everything and not be found out; rationalizing it was a simple task — get the pickup unstuck, clean it up, and get it home before sunrise.

Being highly intoxicated and trying to use my best balance possible, I stood on the edge of the tailgate and tried to jump to the closest dry ground. Jump. Stuck. Yes, I got stuck in the mud. This time, without my red rubber boots. Losing my balance, I fell into the thick mud with my favorite off-white bib overalls that I always wore sporting a colorful tube top. Besides being covered in mud I also lost one of my shoes. I got myself into a terrible situation. My sidekick friend had left and reality was settling into my mind. I was trying to determine what the next step would be since the pickup was not coming out because it was stuck up to the top of the wheels. I would have to walk to get help.

The sky was coal black and I could see the city lights, about three miles away. This helped me figure out how far away I was from the highway. In the distance I caught a glimpse of a yard light from another friend's house. She possibly could help me. The plan was to walk in a straight line to the highway from where the pickup was stuck and then to go to this friend's house. My thinking was, *"If I walk directly towards the highway, I will remember the exact location of where the pickup is stuck."* If I knew the precise position it would help me when I confessed to dad about this fiasco. Walking and at times running with only one shoe made it difficult to keep a straight line to reach my destination. I continually told myself, *"If I look behind me I surely will know the exact spot."* It would make the entire situation more bearable when dad found out.

Once I reached the highway I could not see the pickup it was too far away. I was confident I could remember where it was located. Now, I ran to my friend's house and knocked on her basement bedroom window. She heard me and let me in. I unloaded the whole story. At the end of it she knew I needed more help and was trying to convince me to call my dad and of course, I did not want to. It was becoming light outside, and I knew my original plan of getting it unstuck, cleaned, and back home before sunrise was gone.

I gave in to the idea to call dad to tell him what happened, that it was not that bad and I knew exactly where the pickup was located. The story sure sounded good to me and he seemed to be calm, plus he did not ask, "Why were you driving the pickup in the first place?" I thought to myself, *"Maybe this would not be so bad after all."*

I was confident in directing dad to the exact location of the slough and pickup. Every dirt road we took, we came up empty handed and it could not be found. It seemed like it just disappeared. Dad's burning anger was getting ready to lash out at me. I knew I was too close to the heat because we were sitting in the same vehicle. He was disgusted and ashamed of me so he drove home to try to figure out another plan.

Once home I planned to immediately slip out of the vehicle, into the front door and head straight to the bathroom. I wanted to strip off my dirty clothes, take a shower, and cross the hallway to my bedroom and dive into bed to sleep this night off. There was no such chance of that happening. Dad's anger was building to a rage and I was to feel the wrath. He said, "Get out of the vehicle." He grabbed me by the back of my neck and forced me into the house. He slammed the front door and stood me in front of the key rack that hung behind the door. He proceeded to lift every single key off each hook one by one and said this statement, "You are too dangerous with this," while he lifted the next key and named the vehicle it belonged to. "You are too dangerous with this." Each one, until he got to the riding lawn mower and he said, "And you are even too dangerous with this." I was hoping it was over, but it was not. He took me to the garage and proceeded to find my well packed away ten-speed bicycle. He said, "This is what you'll be driving from now on." No, it could not be true. I hated the ten-speed bike with the skinny narrow tires. We lived two miles out of town on a gravel road and the bike and its skinny tires were no match for the road. I still had a part time job at a pizza joint in town and usually worked nights after school. I told him, "I can't ride the bicycle down the gravel road at night, I might get hit and killed." To that he said, "Good, then I won't have to deal with you anymore."

Dad continued to try to find the pickup with the assistance of additional friends. To no avail, they could not find it. He had to use his last resort, taking his airplane up and flying around in the general area to see if he could find it. Of course, he did. It was farther from the highway than I had remembered. Next, he got a friend who lived close by to use a tractor to pull it out of the field. It was a mess, full of mud and stubble from the cultivated ground. A mess my dad was going to make me clean as an additional part

of my consequences. It took me most of the day at a car-wash to clean the inside and the outside of the pickup. It included cleaning under the hood where the engine was encapsulated in mud from the lame attempt of me trying to get the pickup unstuck.

For the next several weeks I rode the ten-speed bike to and from my job until I could convince some friends to give me rides. It was scary and hard to ride on the gravel road with those silly narrow tires and during that time I thought about how I got myself into the predicament, thinking, *"Maybe, I did have a slight problem?"* I felt bad about this escapade because I should never have taken the pickup. I'm sure dad was humiliated to have a daughter who was constantly in trouble and that everyone in our small community knew about our problems.

Comfy Contract

My self-righteous attitude allowed me to think I could take and use anything of my parents without asking permission, including clothing. Dad had recently bought a comfy down winter jacket and I loved the new chocolate brown color. It was a western cut with a yoke on the back-shoulder area, made of nylon material with dark brown ribbed knit collar and wristbands. I liked it and I knew it would look great one me. I just had to wear it.

Right before leaving the house for a fun-filled time with friends, I decided to wear dad's jacket. At the party I was strutting my stuff and looking fine. It was crowded at the house party with tons of people. It was elbow to elbow with little room to turn. I was smoking, drinking, and having a great time, until a cigarette dropped and landed on the arm of the nylon jacket. It quickly melted a small but noticeable hole in the material; exposing the down feathers. Now I was wishing I had never taken the jacket.

I was never going to confess and tell dad what I had done. It just was not worth the pain. I would wait until he found it and hope I was not at home when he did. It did not take him long. I am sure the lingering aroma of smoke was permeating from the front closet of our house where I hung the jacket as if it was never missing. The smell would have been extremely obvious with parents who did not smoke.

I was home when dad discovered the damaged jacket and he knew I was the culprit. His anger quickly turned to rage. I knew I needed to make a quick escape so I left the house as fast as I could and returned only when I knew the coast was clear after his anger had lifted. The only good thing about dad's anger was that the intensity was quickly extinguished. The anger would subside and he became civil and it was like the situation never happened.

When I came back home he was ready for me with a prepared hand-written contract stating I would be repaying him for the cost of the jacket. It was scribbled on a yellow notepad with a signature line, awaiting my autograph. To me, this was an easy consequence. I quickly signed it and escaped to my bedroom.

Run Away

Run, run, run away! My teenage life was in a tail spin and no one seemed to understand me. My thoughts were constantly twisted in my mind and, mixed with alcohol and drugs, never ended in a good conclusion. I felt extremely hopeless and was not seeking any answers from others who were wiser than me. By myself I determined that running was the answer.

I knew where I would go, to a city several hundred miles away that had an oil boom going on and where my current boyfriend worked. There would be lots of people, action, parties, drugs, and alcohol. Some of my older girlfriends had already left to go live with their boyfriends so it sounded like a fun place to go in my fifteen-year-old mind.

I left after a long night of partying. Instead of driving home I headed out of town. No packing or telling anyone, I just drove off. I thought, *"This will be an attention seeking escapade."* Finally, I would get my parents', mostly my mom's attention. This would show her how much I wanted her attention and needed help.

I headed west early in the morning as the sun was rising and of course, my sidekick was with me and it took over. The last thing I remember seeing is the highway sign two miles out of town. Several hours later when I came to I was maneuvering a curve ten miles north of the oil boom city. The blackout had worn off and I was now in the driver's seat.

My boyfriend was surprised when I arrived unexpectedly yet he was happy to see me. The main objective was to party, nothing more, nothing less. Some of my boyfriends' friends did not like how young I was and were concerned my parents would be sending the cops to find me. I thought mom would report me missing and the cops would track me down in a few days. That never happened. Again, I felt unloved and abandoned. Even these friends did not want me around. The party places changed to the boyfriend's house which was not much fun because there were fewer people. It was all okay for a while because it seemed fun like I was "playing house" while he was working.

I did not have a job so I would hang out with some of the other girlfriends most of the day until he got off work. After a while it began to feel like prison because he started to try to control me and wanted to know my every move, and wanting to know who I was with all the time. His aggressive behavior became violent and after one too many blows I had to leave. I went back home where I did not feel loved or understood.

Prayer Warrior Mom

When mom did not report me as a missing person I was hurt. I thought, *"She must not care about me."* These thoughts confused me and they never left my consciousness. They began to be jumbled up in my mind and became more intense. Each time they rolled around it was an open festering wound. My life was spinning out of control with crazy thoughts. It felt isolating and hopeless because I could not put words out of my mouth to tell mom I wanted help. I was so confused.

Mom was the person who loved me the most during this time. She would tell me she loved me and try and hug me, but I would not let her near me. Never did she give up on me. She decided to do what she was being told by other parents who had lived through crazy times with their teenagers — back off, let go, show tough love, and PRAY!

She was living in her own Hell as a mother watching her first born and only daughter spin out of control. Observing me on a track of recklessness that could lead to death if there was no type of intervention. She and dad had no experience in the type of lifestyle I was living. She did what she knew best, to pray, and ask other faithful prayer warriors to come alongside her and pray me through these tough years.

Manipulation & Men

Manipulation became a game and a way of life for me. It started with my parents and then turned in other directions; inward and with men. My emotions were ice cold and I shut myself off because of the abuse that was happening in this dangerous game. I did not care about myself or anyone else. I was wishing for one guy to like me enough to stay. There were a few guys that seemed to like me enough to truly care. This meant I would finally get what I so desperately seeking, to be liked, but then the game was over. The game became a stronger pull then the true longing of my heart. I would consciously sabotage any relationship that had the possibility of going anywhere.

The craziness of my thinking was taking over the desire of my heart and my soul was becoming dim in the darkness of deception. The deceitful destruction in my mind started with thoughts like: they were not cute enough, they did not have a nice enough car, and they did not have enough money to buy booze or drugs. Then eventually my actions and attitude turned them away. In my dysfunctional thinking, I won the game. Next!

One time I found a guy from Canada who was very nice. He even drove down to the United States to take me on a "real" date. He came into the house and met my parents. I liked him a lot, but I destroyed it just the same. A friend and I drove to Canada, only an hour away, to party and meet him after he got off work. It took him longer than expected to get off work, so we did what was normal activity, drinking and prowling for men. Of course, we found some, and this nice guy who liked me was not too happy. The relationship ended. Next!

There always seemed to be a "next" even though my heart and soul wanted nothing more than to have only one guy who truly cared. The one who paid attention to me, understood me, and truly loved me. This true desire of my heart was overtaken by the game of manipulation, control, and searching to find the best man. The unsatisfied yearning kept me deceived and in the dark where the enemy constantly nipped at my heels. It was a never-ending chase and he never let up.

Mr. Right - Big City Boyfriend

"How would I ever find Mr. Right playing this game?" I believed my girlish dream would eventually come true. My fantasy went back to the fairy tale when I was a little girl in my playhouse. He needed to live in a big city, be adventurous, active, and want to do many fun big city activities. I wanted someone to sweep me off my feet, be financially stable, attractive, and want to spend every minute of his time only with me.

Through a mutual friend, I met a big city guy who was cute and funny. I wanted to get to know him better, but he was not interested in me. That would have to change! My talent of manipulation would help me get what I wanted — the game was on.

I took the opportunity of a rock-n-roll concert at the state fair to get to know him better. I thought to myself, *"This would be my way to get in with him for sure. We can hang out at the concert and then he can give me a ride home."* The comment he made to me was a sure sign I was not on the top of his interest list! In a snide tone, he said, "I'll meet you on the midway!" Hah! — what a blow-off statement! He should have just said, "get lost." I knew he wanted nothing to do with me because he was more interested in my friend, who was a little older, thinner, blonde, and prettier. *"So much for this guy,"* was my thought. NEXT! I still went to the concert with some other friends and we had a great time.

After the concert, those friends and I were walking down the midway of the fairgrounds discussing what our next plans were for the rest of the evening. As I turned my head to respond to a friend I ran smack into someone — BAM! Yep, you guessed it, it was him! We ran into each other on the midway! My response to his surprised and almost disgusted look was, "Hey you said, 'I will meet you on the midway,' so here I am." We hung out the rest of the night and dropped off my pretty friend and shall I say, "the rest is history!" I was sixteen and he was twenty.

I got what I wanted, a big city boyfriend! It would be a challenge to begin the process of stopping the manipulation game in my mind and stay committed to just one guy. This was hard as it meant no more looking around for other men. I wanted to get out of the small town so I knew I had to be committed to one guy. To help this situation I decided in my infamous wisdom to make some changes in my friends. I distanced myself from the older friends and began to hang out with people closer to the same age. It did help and my life began to change. The relationship with the big city boyfriend was good as we began to know each other better by talking on the phone a few times a week. Every weekend I would travel one hundred miles away to see him and spend time together. Our relationship continued to grow and we started to discuss our future together.

Bed Spins

My life was changing for the better because I had a "real" boyfriend but I continued to drink and drug whenever possible. It was difficult to control myself and how much I consumed. I was realizing my dependency on alcohol and drugs were becoming troublesome because it was a common occurrence for me to go home after partying and try sleeping but I would have terrible bed spins. The bed would feel like a spinning merry-go-round that never stopped. When they first started, I could stop them by placing one leg out of the bed and touch my foot on the floor. This technique worked many times, but, just in case it did not, I would always place a garbage can right next to the head side of the bed.

That trick wore off and I needed a new approach to manage this problem. My solution would be to stick my finger in my throat to make myself throw up. It created the extra space needed to have more drinks. I had previously used this method when a great party was happening and I needed more room in my stomach for alcohol. It worked great and allowed me to pass out.

On one occasion of this constant reoccurring scene I began to sob into my pillow out of desperation of my life being a total mess. The wail was deep from my soul. The pain had been welled up in me for so long the sound was excruciating. I thought to myself, *"What is going to happen with my miserable life? All the things people say about me are true. I have no future. I am going to end up pregnant. I may die. My life is a disaster."* I had to stop!

New Friend, Hermit

I knew it would be simple to stop when I had a plan created in my mind. I had to get this "issue" under control. For five years from the age of twelve to seventeen I welcomed alcohol and drugs into my life on a weekly basis. I didn't want to become a "borderline alcoholic" or "drug addict." My strong will power would prove to myself and others I did not need alcohol and drugs to help solve my problems. My solution was to stop and white knuckle this lifestyle.

The plan was to come home right after school and stay home so I would not go out partying with my friends. When I worked at my part time job I would come home directly after work. I studied more and got to know my classmates and my family. It gave me more time to figure out what I wanted for my future since graduation from high school was right around the corner.

For nearly a year my daily agenda was extremely rigid. I went to school, cheerleading practice, basketball games, work, and then home. The relationship with my parents and brothers was good and I maintained a normal teenage lifestyle of watching television and talking to my friends on the phone. On the weekends, I hung out with friends from school. Some of them were beginning to party, but not at the caliber I was used to. I still hung out with them and usually was the designated driver.

This way of living became normal and routine. It seemed like this was standard for other kids my age, I guess? My involvement in extracurricular activities at school became more important than excessive partying. I was in choir, cheerleading, business club, and student council, and was a class officer. I noticed skills and talents I had never known I could do before. Plus, others pointed them out to me.

After a few months, depression set in and I sure did not want *it* as a new friend. I decided to call a friend I had not talked to since I stopped drinking. I wanted to see how she was and what she was doing. Of course, there was a party that night and she asked me if I wanted to go. I thought, *"There was no harm in going to hang out with some old friends who I had only seen in the school hallways for the last year."*

At the party, this guy said, "Come on, you can have just one drink." He proceeded to take a bottle of beer, lifted it close to my face, twisted the cap, it made the "ccchhh" sound of the carbonation being released and I could smell the yeasty, liquid brew. I thought, *"Of course, I can. I will have just one and that will be it."* I wanted to see what it felt like, maybe I would not like the taste or the effect that it had on me. I thought, *"I bet it would taste so good."*

That one drink was not enough, one was never enough, I had to have more. My long-lost friend's alcohol and drugs, quickly found me that night. They would continue to be best friends for the next six years. This time the friendship would be under my terms and we would have to do a better job than before because I now had plans and hope for the future. During the "sober and clean" year I cleared the fog from my mind and I began to realize my entire future was in front of me. I was going to "be somebody" and make a future for myself. Controlling my friends would now be the way we would work this relationship.

Who Cared About Me? Mrs. B.

In the year of clarity, I realized how defensive I was by continuing to push my parents and authority figures far away. I noticed the protective walls and how real they were and how I would not let people get close to me. *Who would ever be able to make an impact on my life and penetrate through the thick high walls?* It did not seem like anyone would be able to get through the "tough" exterior, especially any teacher. My love to learn had been absent for several years, since elementary school. It was more fun to see how I could infuriate teachers and then they would kick me out of class. *The negative attention was at least some attention!*

There was a high school English teacher, Mrs. B, who decided to take a risk with me. She began to show interest in me and over the years would leave a lasting impression on me. I will forever be grateful for her strength, wisdom, and tolerance of having enough patience to love my tough soul during the four years of high school.

She was different than the other teachers; she did not buy into my hate, the outward anger, and the need to try to manipulate every situation. She would challenge my obstinate personality by saying, "I bet you cannot do this or that...." I loved a challenge, so of course I would stick around long enough to show her I could do it. This approach allowed me to stay in her classroom and listen to what she had to say. I liked how she treated all of us, not just me, by giving the whole class little incentives.

When we were good and got our work done we could leave the school and run to the local bakery, which was a few blocks away, to get a treat and then come back before the end of class. She used it as an incentive and a way to build trust. If one of us refused to return to class, all of us would be penalized. We always respected her and followed the rules.

I took every class I could from her and she became my light in a world of darkness. She showed me "tough love" and began to break through my thick walls. She did this by giving me sincere words of encouragement that I had long blocked my ears to hear from any adult. She praised me and acknowledged skills I did not know I had. The simple acts of kindness and words of acknowledgement she invested in me were like giving gold to a poor man. It was during this time of my life when a positive direction for my future seemed dim.

She was good at exposing "the me I was meant to be." She did this by challenging me and at other times sticking up for me. These were all the qualities I so desperately needed to become "something in this world."

One of the talents she saw in me that others did not was my organizational and leadership skills. To expose these, she encouraged me to be the chairperson for our school's prom. She knew I was a born leader, and great at encouraging others to get involved. But I was so fearful to take on such a big challenge that the only way I would do it was if there was another person helping me, so co-chairperson position was created. I accepted the challenge with the goal that it would be much better than any previous prom. It would be memorable and not the same boring way it had always been done. In the past years, the grand march had the couples walking out on the gym floor with ordinary type decorations. I had an extraordinary idea to change things up and make the grand march totally different. We had a stage that was not being used to its fullest so I thought, *"It would be fun if the couples walked on the stage then come through a wooden constructed star then step down a staircase to the gym floor."* Mrs. B was in total support of the idea if we could figure out how to get it accomplished.

Mrs. B, as the teacher advisor for prom, took a lot of heat from other faculty members to let something different happen, especially with me being involved because I was only known for my troubled past. I do not know if we truly realized how much  she put herself on the line for us. She always kept a calm, matter-of-fact attitude around the students so we never could tell how much pressure this may have caused.

She was fun, encouraging, and always challenging us to be who we believed we were to be. She personally risked her reputation by sticking up for me several times. This showed me I could trust her and know she truly had my back. She is the one person who was instrumental in my attending college and becoming a leader in so many areas of my life.

I enjoyed every minute of being the prom co-chairperson and began to visualize myself doing things I never could imagine. I recognized some talents and skills in myself and if I was persistent they could become positive traits. I believed I did a good job as the co-chairperson and others did too because I received many compliments. The best gift

I got for this project was personally delivered to my house by Mrs. B. She delivered a beautiful bouquet of flowers and a card saying, "Thanks for all the hard work." Those few simple words would sink deep in my heart and be part of the chisel that begin to break down a portion of my wall.

Negative Attention

The other teachers and authorities did not rank too high in my mind. I got a thrill out of butting heads with them to get attention, though negative, and I did get noticed. I could not seem to stop the negative behaviors and be recognized for any talents I had developed. A rebel reputation was a dark shadow which followed me everywhere I went.

Most adults — parents, teachers, probation officer, and law enforcement — viewed me as a "trouble maker with a capital T." Their eyes were on me whenever I was around, for a good reason. My parents, watched me because of the extensive list of conflicts they had with me daily: the drinking, drugging, staying out late for days, running away, destroying their property, stealing money, charging gas to their account, the list was endless. Other parents did not want their children around me, because of the bad influence I would have on them, and warn their kids not to hang out with me. They knew my reputation based on what they read in the local newspaper or from what they heard from students talking at school.

Other teachers and the principal watched me like a hawk because I regularly created mischief in class. I liked to provoke other students to help me with whatever scheme I had for the day. One incident was taking dog shark remains we had dissected in biology class and hiding them behind a history teacher's desk. He was annoying and a boring teacher. Most of the students did not like him either, so he was a good target. We pulled off the prank, but one thing I did not think through was how horrible the smell would be to all of us before it was found out.

As far as the principal, we were on a first name basis. I knew exactly what the inside of his office looked like because I was sent there weekly, if not daily for many minor issues. The more severe ones, like in-school suspension, I would have to stay in his office for the entire day. I was suspended for smoking cigarettes while wearing my cheerleading uniform. Another one was for swearing at a teacher. He was firm and strict because during his many years as principal he had dealt with others like me. He was also a wise man. During my senior year, he highly recommended, if nearly forcing me, to take as many college classes at our community's junior college to keep me out of trouble at high school. I did not want to take any classes there, it would mean I would have to pay attention and do some real work. There were several older friends and my parents that made it sound appealing so I decided it couldn't hurt me to take a few classes. In two years I took three college level classes equaling fifteen credits.

To sum up my high school years, academically, I was an average student and when I paid attention I would pull

A's and B's. From my parents' perspective, it was a terrible troubling time and one they could not wait to be finished. I did graduate from high school. I was ready to leave the small town and never come back.

On graduation day after the ceremony and saying goodbye to many friends, it was my one and only goal to leave. Before I could go there was a small gathering of family at the house to open the cards, eat cake, and visit. My favorite gift from my parents, a three-piece set of suitcases. I packed them as full as possible with as many of my possessions as I could stuff into the "suitcases of freedom." I was packing with the intent of never returning. With my bags packed and my big city boyfriend helping me, we walked out the doors. I was college bound, off to my new life, a life with no parents and other authority figures breathing down my neck. I had no intentions to ever return. My new home would be with my boyfriend, my life on my own was just beginning. The girlish dream brought a glimmer of hope into my life again because I was leaving the past behind, it would be a fresh start!

REFLECTION PAUSE

My life shattered when I was uprooted from the small-town school and put into a much larger school setting during Christmas break of sixth grade. It felt like my world was crumbling down around me. Knowing only one single person in the new community who was a few years older put me at a troubling start. This was the beginning of a lasting habit of hanging out with much older people. It was a trap that snagged me for years. This exposed me to alcohol and drugs that became my primary focus. It created many problems for me and my family. The more I drank and used drugs the more I did not care about my family. It was the darkest part of my life.

Things happened to me that cannot be written about without hurting more people. It is best to let your mind only imagine the places and things because it is a time when I flirted with the enemy in the closest way possible every day. Some of you know exactly the kind of places and things that happened to me without the need to describe them, only because you have been there yourself.

I hated God because I had a limited understanding of Him. The only thing I was sure of was what my parents and other adults told me about God and that I would be condemned for all my bad behaviors. I did not know how to change because I kept everyone pushed away with the walls of protection I built. I would not let anyone help me. The one and only glimmer of hope of reaching me, with a true understanding of God, was during my short stint in confirmation class. This went terrible and spiraled into a nightmare when the pastor told me I would go to Hell. Those words replayed a million times in my head convincing me I was in Hell and there was no way out. I concluded I would continue the destructive path and try to make the best of a terrible situation.

The confirmation class situation I used as the reason to profess I was an atheist. Years later, I would classify myself as an agnostic, a person who claims they cannot have true knowledge about the existence of God but does not deny God might exist. Whenever the opportunity presented itself I expressed my opinions about my belief and this so-called God. It led to a journey of confusion that took years to repair. I created a perfectly good and justifiable resentment towards the church and this God. It gave me every reason to do the exact opposite of the "goody two shoes lifestyle." I had more fun with my friends, alcohol, and drugs, who were my companions for years.

In my young teenage mind, there was a lot of confusion and conflict because I felt no one loved me, especially not my parents. I believed this after my cry for help was not heard when I ran away from home. They never sent the cops to find me or report me miss-

ing and this made me feel unloved and as if I was a low priority. Even the boyfriend who said he loved me was not quite enough for me to believe that he truly loved me. There were too many past experiences with men that had gone wrong to ever allow me to truly think someone loved me.

It would take approximately thirty years to understand the complexity of my feelings of not feeling loved. During a healing stage of life, God revealed to me how I needed to put myself in my mother's shoes and try to imagine what I put them through as parents. As a mother of my own children I now can understand. I have shed many cleansing tears from my aching soul and broken heart because of the revelation of the pain my parents endured. God helped me make sense of the pain in myself and the pain I created for my parents, especially my mom. I was understanding how I felt as an "unloved teenage girl" at the same time acknowledging how my mom felt as a "mother of an unruly, lost girl."

Mom did the best she knew how in a terrible situation. In her anger, she said things that pushed me further away and by pushing everyone away I built my walls of protection in reaction to the hurtful words. This was the time when mom started the "tough love" and when I ran away from home. They happened to coincide with each other and ended with the result of more confusion and rebellion on my part.

I strongly believe in God's timing and that nothing happens in God's world by mistake. While I was running away and feeling the most unloved, mom was taking care of herself and praying for me. By practicing "tough love" and saying many prayers for me, she became stronger. Mom's faithful prayers over the years were always heard by God. She also recruited others to pray. She asked every month at the women's meeting to please keep praying for me, to keep me safe, alive, and to be set free.

I can attest that even though I lived through many years of craziness and darkness I was protected from many unfathomable situations that could have happened to me. I believe it was all because of a faithful, praying mother and her friends who never gave up, and their belief I would finally find God.

Realization Years

 This is what I
REMEMBER
from this time
IN MY LIFE...

Playing House Again

Setting up our first apartment was like playing
house when I was a young girl in the back yard on
the farm — it was fun, new each time, and something I had in my control. It reminded me of my
playhouse days when I would rearrange furniture
to make it fit just right, buying groceries, and cooking delicious meals. The mud and grass soup along
with the play dough pies had now become mac-
aroni and cheese, tuna, and maybe a boxed cake.
When we started out we had very little, even the
little things to get started, like salt, pepper, flour,

sugar, toilet paper, and laundry detergent. There sure wasn't much excitement in buying all these necessities to start our life on our own.

My boyfriend was everything I knew he would be from my dreams. He was good looking, had a nice car, a good job, treated me well, and truly seemed to like me. *I am glad he did, because I did not like myself.* As life went on and we lived together with no firm commitment in our relationship the excitement stage moved to the familiar and critical stage. Individual habits we both did became noticeable and annoying. The dream of getting swept off my feet slowly disappeared and other activities needed to fill the space where the girlish daydreams were going awry. The primary focus was parties and friends.

We both had jobs and were committed to being self-sufficient and successful. I attended a four-year university determined to make something of myself and prove to my dad and every other adult from my small-town I was going to be somebody. My daily schedule was full of school, homework, and a part-time job. Going to school from eight a.m. to noon, then to work for six to eight hours, studying until midnight, and repeating it over again for several years until I graduated. Parties and the bar scene were only allowed on the weekend, otherwise it took a toll on my hectic schedule. I controlled my desire to become too chummy with alcohol and drugs by staying busy.

My boyfriend was a blue-collar guy. He was five years older than me and had worked for a few years at his job.

His focus was to party most every night of the week. He seemed to be able to handle it well and only stayed at the bar until a little after supper time most days. By the time I would get off work in the early evening he would be home. I thought, *"He was very attentive to be home to greet me when I got off work."*

Our first apartment was nice and cozy, it was an efficiency apartment. We had very few possessions when we moved in as it only took one trip up the flight of stairs to get all our belongings situated. All we had was a lawn chair, and a plastic milk crate, which was used as a stand for our twelve-inch black and white television. We eventually bought a used couch and chair, a waterbed, and a few other pieces of furniture to make it our own place. It was fun playing house; cooking, cleaning, and being away from our parents.

Alcohol and drugs were frequently invited over, especially on the weekends. Even though I worked and went to college, I managed to maintain a good performance at both. I controlled my friends, alcohol, and drugs, because I needed to stay focused and achieve my goals. These friends continually hung around and were the primary focus of our attention for many years. We both kept our jobs with only a few consequences from our close friends. We settled into a routine of going to work, paying bills, and having fun on the weekend.

Did You Say, Married?

We were approaching close to five years of being together and had talked many times about making it legal and getting married. I was always waiting for him to ask the question. Then one day it finally happened; I was sitting on the couch and he said he wanted to ask me something. He knelt by me and put his hand behind the pillow that was tucked behind my back and where he had hidden a box. He pulled out a box, which he opened and exposed a beautiful diamond ring and said, "Will you marry me?" Of course, my answer was yes!

Now it was time to plan the biggest party of our lives! Since we had been living together for five years it was all about the party because it would be a celebration of making it officially legal. The wedding date was set on the five-year anniversary of our first date. We wanted a traditional wedding; wedding dress, bridesmaids, groomsmen, tuxes, family, food, dancing; oh yeah, and to make it official we needed to have it in a church. Neither of us had been brought to church regularly as children so we decided to ask the church his mom attended.

The church wedding seemed like the proper thing to do and everyone else was getting married in a church. We had no other reason, it sounded like a good place to have the ceremony. Before we could get married in the church we needed to visit with the priest, who said every couple was required to do several sessions of marriage counseling. *Wow!* This would be interesting. We had been living together for five years and were two very strong independent thinkers. Plus, we both had a limited understanding of God and we wondered what type of questions he would ask.

The sessions began. They involved various subjects a husband and wife will encounter during married life: communication, finances, and children and parenting. I clearly recall the time we talked about finances. Our plan as we entered marriage was to pay for everything evenly, the 50/50 rule; "Even Steven" was our motto. If we needed to come together financially we would, but only if it was necessary. We would continue to keep separate checking accounts and have only the major purchases in both of our names. The priest doing the sessions was trying to communicate the pros and cons to our way of thinking, but we wanted nothing to do with his viewpoint. It never crossed our minds that any negatives would arise out of our way of doing things.

Once the sessions ended we were on our way to being married in a church with all the religious customs that came with it. With the guidance of the priest, we were to organize the ceremony and select scriptures to be read at the wedding. Only rarely had either of us touched a Bible, let alone read or understood anything it said to be at all able to select a few scriptures. Choosing would be based purely on secular and personal beliefs or the way it sounded when we read them out loud. After the priest made a few recommendations, we were to go home and review them and make our final selection.

I found the Bible mom gave me years before and began trying to find and read the verses the priest suggested. I was furious! Many of them, if not all, had the "O word."

Absolutely *no* way would I let the "O word" be read! I already told my soon to be husband we would *not* be reading them during our wedding. I was ornery, this isn't the "O word," and stubborn. He just laughed and knew I would never be the "O word" type of wife, the word I am referring to is... *obedient*!

I made sure of it, in very plain language to the priest, that none of those scriptures with the word obedient were to be read at our wedding. I was a woman of the 1980's and was not going to be under a husband's thumb and be obedient. For heaven sakes, if they were read at the wedding it could mean I would have to do what it said or be what it was referring to in the words. Not me!

It was a nice, traditional church wedding with all the components to make it look totally put together. The focus was on after the wedding — the party! There was a live band, a keg of beer, food, and many friends. It was all we expected and I did not want the night to end. Just like the many other times of big parties I never wanted the night to end. When it was coming to the end, my now husband wanted to go home and I did not want to stop partying. Friends were going out for breakfast at the truck stop, which was one of my favorite after-party places to go eat a gut bomb breakfast and I wanted to go with them. Besides, we were not going on a honeymoon so why would it matter if I went with them? I lost out on the idea of hanging out with friends at the truck stop and we went home.

Since we were going home and the night was ending I thought once we got to our front door he should pick me up and carry me over the threshold. It was raining outside and I was already a mess after spilling an entire bottle of pink champagne on my wedding dress, but he did it anyway. In we came to our house, to life as it had already been for several years. Nothing was different, except I was wearing a wedding dress and now had a ring. All I could think about was the things I would miss by not going to the truck stop. That is not what my new husband had in mind, but that is what was on my mind, making myself breakfast before going to bed. Just like many nights in the past, drinking, partying, and passing out, it would be the same on this night.

Mr. and Mrs.

It was official, we were legally husband and wife. I would be graduating with a four-year degree and pursuing a career in the business world. He was busy working hard so we could buy our first house and vehicle along with many other things we wanted as a young married couple.

We settled into a rhythm of working all week and usually waiting until the weekend to party. Most weeks we were good and held off until the weekend, other weeks were not

as good. Alcohol and drugs were truly good friends and hung around us often. I had taught myself how to control my drinking and using. It was much different than it was in high school because I had more responsibilities and I wanted a better life for my future. I knew what had got me into trouble before so I would not do those same things. By making a firm decision to seek out help when needed. My gauge of severity of when I would know I needed help was if I ever started drinking or using alone. I loved parties and being around others whenever I drank, so I knew that if I began doing these things by myself, then I truly had a problem.

Things started to catch up with us as we began to have several close calls with alcohol and drugs in getting caught, with dire consequences being the result. I began to ponder the merit to the statement that constantly stayed in my mind from my teenage years when I got the DUI, *"Was I a borderline alcoholic? What was that anyway?"* I never gave it much thought before now because I simply did not want to be an alcoholic or drug addict. If I admitted it, I would need to get help and make major changes in my life.

There was nothing in my life that was ever borderline. I was either in or out, black, or white, I never sat in the middle. I either was an alcoholic or I was not! I let the question linger in my mind and reviewed my years of friendship with alcohol and drugs. It was an interesting relationship, with many severe consequences. I justified I had no true dependence but I decided to limit the time I spent with them. In examining my usage, I also started reviewing my husband's relationship with our "friends." It was much easier to look at him than at myself. His connection with them was way closer than mine, maybe he had more of a problem than me. The haunting statement continued to play in my head, *"borderline alcoholic."* I was getting worn-out of being "sick and tired" and wanted a clear answer to this taunting statement.

This need took me into action to search for clarity on the label I was being tagged with by visiting a professional counselor about all my other problems — husband, childhood, and possibly my friendship with alcohol and drugs. After several sessions of explaining my issues the counselor asked me to answer a ten-point questionnaire rating my need to depend on alcohol. I viewed them as trick questions. I felt I answered appropriately to get the results I was looking for: that I was *not* an alcoholic. But six out of ten answer results told me I may have an alcohol dependency issue.

My immediate conclusion was the counselor did not know what she was talking about, leading me to find another one who would understood my issues. The new counselor offered the same alcohol dependence questionnaire and this time thought I knew exactly how to answer to get the results

I wanted. Yet, this time I got eight out of ten answer results indicating an alcohol dependence. Clear, right? No. They did not understand. How I viewed it was my husband was the one who had a worse problem than me. This counselor suggested I try attending a twelve-step program for family members of people who have alcohol dependence issues.

Ah ha! Now they were speaking my language. I *knew* it was my husband who had the issue, not me. Off I went to get involved with this program. I liked it and could relate a little too much. After a year of attending regular weekly meetings and working with a sponsor to learn how to detach from my husband's problems my sponsor dropped a bomb on me. I was on the phone with her complaining and having a hard time understanding why things were not changing with my relationship with my husband. She turned the conversation around and said, "Have you ever looked at your drinking?" Oh, boy, now that set my anger off! How dare she be so blunt, rude, and judgmental. I had had enough of her and this program.

I tromped back to the counselor to spill my guts about all the injustice I had endured in the last year. After a few sessions, she brought up those results of the alcohol questionnaire I took the year before. She was also blunt, rude, and judgmental, telling me, "I needed to take care of my issues and not my husband's." I could not escape from this issue, it was coming at me from all sides, I finally surrendered and admitted I had a problem with alcohol and drugs.

No borderline alcoholic, no looking at my husband, I needed to do something about *my* issues and get off the blame game. I had to surrender and be done. My last drink was March 17, 1990. I decided to go to outpatient alcohol and drug treatment, which included several months of after care. I was excited and totally committed and ready to live a new way of life. I hoped my husband would also decide to change along with me. Nope. That was *not* the case. He was *very* angry and wanted absolutely nothing to do with what I had decided. His drinking buddy was gone and he did not like it.

Bye, Bye Old Friends

My focus was to strip away the wreckage of the past. I needed to understand how I could *control* my drinking and using, not necessarily stop entirely. If I stopped completely I would not have a husband, or anymore fun, plus I did not know any other lifestyle.

During treatment, counselors told me to change the people, places, and things that surrounded me that made me want to drink and use. That seemed truly impossible because I was only twenty-three-years old; my life was just starting. I could not imagine changing my life that much. What would I do with all this free time? One counselor mentioned a few activities I may want to think about doing: bowling or photography. The look on my face was that of, "You have to be kidding me!" There was *no* way I would go bowling or buy a camera to take pictures. I still wanted to have fun, hang out with my friends, and have a good time. All they needed to do was teach me how to keep myself under control and not to drink to the state of blacking out.

Treatment was the first time I looked at my drinking and using on paper in black and white by doing a usage chart and it was a shock and a reality check. Being so young I thought it would be easy to complete because I only drank for eleven years. It was hard to look at all the times I drank, give the estimated quantity consumed each of those times, and the consequences of my drinking and using during each of those times. My eyes were finally opened to how bad my life had gotten.

Listening to others who were in treatment and those at the twelve-step programs helped me begin to realize I was not unique. I could understand and relate more and more, seeing and hearing more similarities than differences. The thought of finding the answer to my crazy problems started to make sense.

The first few years of living a sober and clean with no relationship with my old friend's alcohol and drugs were very hard, if not close to impossible. My husband wanted his party buddy back and he would try anything in his power to sabotage my sobriety. It was miserable and hard to live this new way of life. I distanced myself from him and sank deep into service work in the twelve-step program to find any and every reason to not be around him and the lifestyle he continued to live.

At about two years of staying sober and clean I had enough of being around my husband's lifestyle and wanted to leave the relationship. A divorce would be easy and clean because we had no children, one house, and one new vehicle. I desperately wanted out and was willing to simply walk away; just split the sheets, a clean deal, no harm to each other, we needed to be done! The two years of living very separate lives had taken a heavy toll on my heart. We were not much more than roommates and no signs of improvement.

During this time of planning my escape and sharing frustrations, women I got to know through the twelve-step program encouraged me to consider helping to carry the message of hope from the disease of addiction to my husband. One of them said, "You cannot just walk away from him. You must carry the message of what this twelve-step program has to offer." My reply to her was, "Oh, yes I can walk away. Let someone else carry the message." I thought, *"That response will stop her from thinking I would do such a crazy thing."* She was not done with me, she gave me a challenge. She said, "Get down on your knees in prayer for two weeks and pray for your husband." The suggestion was for me to pray for him as if I was praying for myself; all the good things I wanted for myself, I was to pray for him. After two weeks of praying for him daily, if I still felt like I could walk away without carrying the message, then I could leave.

It was also advised to add a prayer to lift the veil of darkness from his eyes. Hmm, I had no idea what these ladies were talking about, but I respected them and wanted what they had in their lives. I accepted the challenge and tried my hardest to do what they told me.

Since I was in the beginning stages of learning about prayer and meditation, it was confusing. Prayer was talking to my Higher Power and meditation was listening. I was doing a whole lot of talking and needed to do more listening. The prayers being said to a Higher Power felt odd and uncomfortable because I had no relationship with a god.

Each night for two weeks I got down on my knees beside our bed and prayed for all the things I wanted: to stay sober and clean, to understand the twelve-step program as a way of life, to love and be kind to other people, to be able to look at myself and start loving myself, and to begin changing character defects in myself. Lastly, to lift the veil of darkness from his eyes. This entire process was so confusing, *"How can any of this work?"*

Twelve to fourteen days later I reported back to the women and told them, "I guess my heart is softened slightly. I am willing to carry the message, but merely as another member of the program, then I am going to divorce him." My response was not warm and fuzzy, more matter-of-factly because I had no feelings left for him, our marriage seemed hopeless and not salvageable. As a member of the twelve-step program I would do my best and carry the message to him that there was another way to live his life.

The suggested way to carry the message was to do an intervention. I agreed and set a date for an early Sunday morning with the plan to have a male and female addiction counselor come to our house and help me communicate how his drinking and using had affected our marriage.

As I was waiting for the date to arrive I began some new prayers. Prayers to have my husband continue his heavy drinking and using and be *very* hung over for the morning of the intervention. Of late, that did not seem to be a problem since he was out partying with friends most every night. I also prayed for my emotions to come back into my heart and to have descriptive words to share with him how his drinking and using had affected me and our marriage.

The day was fast approaching and my feelings were like ice cubes regarding how things had affected me. There was nothing left in my heart, the feelings were so removed and I was disengaged. This seemed like a confirmation that a divorce was inevitable. I would go through this process of an intervention and just act like any other member who was simply carrying the message of hope and a possible way out of the addictions.

The night before the counselors were to arrive early in the morning, I was home alone like I was most nights. This was a good sign that one prayer would be answered — he was out with his friends, and a hangover was guaranteed. As for the other prayer of getting my emotions back in my heart and having descriptive words to express myself on how his drinking and using had affected us, that was not happening. I decided to distract myself with cleaning, it kept me busy and time passed quickly. I was getting myself prepared and organized for the next phase of life. I needed to be ready to leave, file the divorce papers, and find a place of my own to live. While sorting through random papers I found some notes my husband had written me about his drinking and using and how it had made him be a person he did not want to be, that he was sorry and thought he may have a problem. These notes were the answer to my prayer to having descriptive words about how his drinking and using had affected our marriage. His own words would be read to him as he lay in bed very hung over with two addiction counselors, one on each side of the bed, and me at the foot of the bed.

Stunned is an extremely mild word to use as to how he reacted to the guests who were present in our bedroom that early morning in the fall of 1992. Anger was the next visible reaction of which he was now wide awake and had moved himself into the living room. I had done my part of the intervention by reading the letters I found. Now the counselors took over and did what they do best. It was an interesting hour or so with many hurtful words said. He eventually agreed to go to treatment.

"Good riddance" was my thought with a mental kick in the rear end as he walked out the door with the two counselors. I went back to cleaning and trying to figure out what my future would hold. I was done and simply needed to move on.

About two weeks after he left for treatment I received a phone call from him asking me to bring him a pair of socks. *"Socks? What? Don't they give you a nice pair of hospital socks?"* I told him, "Sure I can drop some off." I went to the nurses' station at the treatment center to drop off the socks and intended to simply give them to the nurse and leave. As I turned to exit the center I heard my name called by my husband, he said "Wait, I want to talk to you." We had not talked in a civil manner for at least a year. I stood there staring at him, wanting to run or shout with anger at the top of my lungs because I did not know what to say or how to respond. I looked at him with a blank expression and said, "What?" With the sincerest look and tone in his voice he said, "Thank you. Thank you for getting me some help."

Walls Crumble

The protective walls from my childhood were still standing and hiding my broken heart that was full of pain. At times, I would cry out because my life seemed so utterly hopeless. The crying was like light penetrating the thick walls, awakening my emotions. Many times, I would break down crying out in more frustration, anger, and exhaustion saying, "If there is a God, *help me*, please *help me!*" I had no other options but to cry out. This was the beginning of breaking down the brick and mortar in my walls and they had started to crumble.

This God I cried out to for *help* was foreign to me. I had no true knowledge of Him because I had pushed Him far away. I surely did not think He would help me, nor would He hear me. As I sat there in pure exhaustion, I heard a still small voice, sounding like I was talking to myself, *"It will be okay."* At that instant, I felt something I had never experienced, it was the most indescribable peace that came over me. It felt like someone came and poured oil all over me, it was comforting and soothing, it made me motionless, frozen in the moment.

The emotions that were held up in me for years came pouring out as tears of relief. I finally surrendered and let go of my self-centered determination to try and stay in control. It had disappeared. This God that others spoke of was giving me relief and peace. He was doing something to me I could not conceive nor understand. I was in awe at the knowledge that there truly had to be a God who loved me.

For I know the plans I have for you, declares the Lord,
plans to prosper you and not harm you,
plans to give you hope and a future.

[JEREMIAH 29:11 NIV]

This was the first day I came to believe in the one true God, the one who was going to help me. It was the beginning step into a personal relationship with God, of knowing Him in a way I heard others talk about. It was not the same God who I was told would condemn me for the rest of my life. He was someone I could start to trust and try to love.

The sense of peace I experienced while hearing the still, small voice had such an impact on me that it turned my ways of darkness to light. The high, dark walls I hid behind were falling apart. I wanted freedom from the fortress I had locked myself in, ridding myself of the activities, places, and people where darkness hid. Just like it says in the book of Peter:

...for he called you out of the darkness
into his wonderful light.

[1 PETER 2:9 NLT]

The light of God outshines any amount of darkness. On that day, at that moment, the light showered down on my ungodliness, emptiness, torture, loneliness, isolation, and abandonment — it forever changed my life!

He brought them out of darkness
and the deepest gloom
and broke away their chains.

[PSALM 107: 14 NIV]

Changes began to happen because I was exposed to this light of God. New people were coming into my life, and friendships were developing. They were nice people and they wanted to get to know me and always greeted me with a hug. It was such a new and different feeling for me to have physical hugs from others. In the past, I didn't like hugging, it was way too close in my physical boundary. It involved close contact and entailed letting them into the walls of protection.

It took time but the thick bricks in the two layered walls that I created slowly began to come down. The hugs of several loving and patient women penetrated the slight cracks in the outer wall. As for the inner most wall that surrounded my heart, it too began to crumble from my heart, feeling and sensing the love being showered on me. The well-established inner wall was one I decided to break down and push out of the way.

The close interaction was new and awkward, it felt like these women were invading my space. It was surreal to have them approach me with open arms for a hug. I taught myself to not back up and walk away from this new physical contact. They were helping and guiding me into a new way of living and loving. I had nothing to lose and everything to gain because I was on a new journey with God. He was carrying me. I needed to trust Him and believe this experience was okay, to know His love and to depend on His help.

One woman would hug, squeeze, and kiss me on the cheek. At first, it was terribly uncomfortable but every time I saw her she would do this same thing. Eventually it started to feel so warm and comforting I could hardly wait to see her the next time. The hugs from a stranger, now becoming a friend, helped break down years of coldness, not feeling, and isolation. She kept on hugging and loving me for several more years until I could fully accept hugs and hug others. This is when I can say, without a shadow of a doubt, "God's love had truly penetrated my heart."

As John 7:38 CSB states,

> *The one who believes in me,*
> *as the Scripture has said,*
> *will have streams of living water*
> *flow from deep within him.*

Did You Say, Children?

My focus turned to my career and how I was going to climb the corporate ladder in the business world. I was constantly seeking the approval of my dad in becoming a successful business woman. It was very important for me to show him I could become a somebody he could be proud of and not the troubled teenage girl stuck in his memory. I was incessantly focused on my dad's approval.

I was a woman of the 1980's where "I am woman, hear me roar" was spoken loud and clear. Women were told to stand up for their rights, make yourself known, climb the corporate ladder with men, demand the same salary, do not give an inch to your feminine side, and fight until the bitter end. This thinking can make for one fierce, tough exterior of a woman and one who will do most anything to keep the corporate position she had attained.

I heard the message plainly and did what needed to be done to get to the top rung of the ladder. At times, I pushed others aside not concerned about them or their feelings. I would take the politically correct side of an opinion to keep on the right side of the fence, even if it was not my belief. I was taught how to fight the fight amongst men making sure all my emotions were constantly in check as to not show any weakness. There was to be no weak links in

the chain. I had to remain solid if I was going to keep the status and clout in the corporate environment amongst men.

All the climbing and fighting to get to the top in the company took tons of energy and focused attention. There was no spare time for children. They did not seem to fit neatly into my clearly defined career plans. Children would only side track me and create more of a juggling act.

I had very little interest in having children. The nurturing, mothering gene in me was a weak one. I had helped care for my brothers at a very young age and it allowed me enough insight to know I was not interested in children. There was too much responsibility to go along with them and I did not want twenty plus years full of headaches and turmoil. A cold thought, but the truth!

My focus for life was to have a successful career and lots of money in the bank, then my life would be complete. This would show everyone I had arrived and just who I was, a successful girl from a small town who had many troubles as a youth, now a successful business woman. In this narrow view, I targeted my eyes on climbing the ladder of success, even if it meant showing others up to get to the next rung. The carrot was set in front of me and no one could stop me. I had no other responsibilities outside my career so climbing the corporate ladder was my number one goal.

Children were not high on my list of priorities. My attitude was one of, *"I will let you know when I am ready to have children."* I was a woman in control of her life, her body and yes, her husband. My old friend, manipulation, and I began to chum around when it came to the "having children" issue with my husband. I would be the one to decide when to have children, if ever. Not him! I made sure he knew I was in control of my body and he was not. To make this point clear several times I would say, "I will never have children." It was mean and cold-hearted, yet it communicated my thought very clearly. End of story, no more discussion.

My husband continued to nag and prod me about his desire to have children; it was annoying. I was tired and getting worn down with this constant pressure and finally gave in at a weak moment, and said, "Okay, just one child. I can handle one." I was overseeing a multimillion dollar department within a company I worked for, and surely, I could deal with one child. My rationale was that one child would not hurt the whole process or side track my career goals.

Early Arrival

Once my mind was made up to try to have a child I believed it would happen right away and the process could move along. Six years later hopelessness set in because there were no blue lines appearing on the pregnancy stick. Every month was torture to think, *"Now I cannot have children. There must be something wrong with me?"* Adoption became the next topic of discussion and both of us were not quite convinced. The age clock was ticking as we were both climbing in years. Now that I was sold on the idea of having a child, nothing was happening. Then one day in 1993

I knew something was different and sure enough the blue line appeared on the stick. Excitement was racing in my heart, we had been ready and waiting for this day for years and it had finally arrived.

This *"mom thing"* was not going to be as bad as I had thought. Being older and having a few years established in my career I felt I could handle whatever was thrown my way. Month by month I followed along in a wonderful book describing in detail the amazing creation being formed within me, a new life we would raise together in this world.

One of the hobbies we never gave up while I was pregnant was riding motorcycle. I even took my driving portion of the motorcycle test while I was five months pregnant. The doctor visits for checkups were going well and all was normal. During the six-month checkup, I asked the doctor if it was okay to continue riding motorcycle for the last few months. The doctor did not like the idea and suggested I stop driving, but I could occasionally ride as a passenger. The summer plans would need a slight change after this news. Shortly we would be off on a long trip with our motorcycle friends to the 90th Anniversary of Harley Davidson in Milwaukee, Wisconsin. Instead of riding the motorcycle I would be the driver for the pilot vehicle in our pickup with the entire group's luggage. It was disappointing but I wanted to follow the doctors' orders and be careful.

One month after the Milwaukee trip we took another one closer to home to the HOG (Harley Owners Group) Rally within the state. I did the same as the other trip and was the pilot vehicle driver. This time I did get to do a little riding once we arrived, it was the end of August and beautiful weather. We enjoyed a few short rides along with visiting the many friends we came to know through the years.

Being very active in the HOG we and our friends were volunteering for registration at the rally. It was fun because you would see everyone who was coming to the event. Being in my seventh month of pregnancy and visibly pregnant many people commented and asked when the baby was due and if we were going to name it Harley? My response was, "The due date is October 10th and, no, we are not naming the baby Harley!"

The end of the first day of the rally we were done with the registration and ready to go eat supper. The restaurant was a short distance so we rode the motorcycle. My husband and I arrived early and waited in the center square area of the beautiful quaint tourist town to meet up with the rest of the group. It was Saturday, August 28th, a very hot, humid day. It was great riding weather but terribly hot since I was big and pregnant. As I was sitting on a bench waiting for the others, I was thinking, *"The baby would be arriving in about seven or eight weeks and next week we start Lamaze classes. The room is ready with a Winnie the Pooh theme, clothes and diapers are bought, and the names were picked out."* We were so excited for a boy or girl to join us and to come to the end of being pregnant into the beginning of a new life for all of us.

My husband had walked over to a store across the street to look around and burn up time, while I stayed on the bench watching people. I noticed how hard and firm my abdomen had become and some mild back pain started. I stood up to relieve the pressure and pain and I was instantly surprised by what felt like a garden hose being turned on in my pants. I had never wet my pants before, and this was beyond embarrassing! Looking frantically for my husband and not seeing him anywhere close by, fear began to set in and I froze solid, not wanting to move. The least bit of movement to turn and look for him brought another gush and the reality of what was happening. My water had broken and I was at the end of my thirty-second week of pregnancy. I knew this was bad and something was wrong. Water breaking — seven weeks early — away from home on the motorcycle — husband off looking in a store — and there I stood utterly embarrassed because my pants were soaked with liquid running down my legs. *"What was I going to do?"*

My husband appeared and said, "What is wrong?" *"He could not see what was happening?"* I felt like I was standing in a puddle of water. When I looked down there was no pool surrounding my feet. *"Maybe I was imagining things, maybe not. I was a smart woman. I needed to get my thoughts collected and calm down."*

The store my husband just came from is where we headed to see if I could use the bathroom. I patiently stood in line behind a customer making a purchase; rehearsing in my mind what I would say to this middle-aged woman I had never met. My husband had left me there to quickly take the motorcycle back to the hotel and bring the pickup back to get me. It was finally my turn, the lady said, "How can I help you?" I responded, "Can I use the bathroom?" She replied, "I am sorry. We do not have public bathrooms." A second, more drastic attempt was needed, I said, "I am seven months pregnant and my water broke. Can I use your bathroom while my husband goes to get our pickup?" That did it! The lady quickly turned and came rushing around the counter and put her arms around me and escorted me down the hallway to the bathroom.

I was so scared and nervous as I sat on the toilet in a strange bathroom realizing my water broke. My mind started darting madly. *"What if the baby was coming? I wondered if it can be stopped. What if the baby is in danger?"* My mind could not stop. I had not read that far in the book and purposely did not read the emergency section because it was not going to happen to me. *"Was I in danger too? Oh man, there were more questions than answers."* I started crying, the fear was taking over, or maybe it was shock setting in. Just then I heard a knock on the door, it was the lady asking, "Are you okay? Can I come in?"

By her looks, she was in her late fifties, and now very motherly, not the lady of a few minutes ago, with her business face on saying, "No, we do not have public restrooms." She was concerned and helped me to stay calm by asking questions to distract me. We visited about small details like when was my due date, if this was our first child, and where we were from. She calmed me down and kept me from projecting too far into the immediate future. Another knock on the bathroom door and it was my husband, visibly shaken and not sure what to do next.

I did not want to leave the safety of the four walls of the bathroom, yet I realized I needed medical help. My husband and the woman helped walk me out to the pickup. I continued to feel liquid running down my legs and pain happening in close intervals. We needed to get to the closest larger community for help because it was a small tourist town with no large medical facility available to adequately care for my situation.

Before leaving for the hospital we quickly went back to the hotel to talk to one of the ladies in our riding group who was a registered nurse and worked in obstetrics. She assured us that, yes, the baby would be coming soon, that I was in labor and I needed to keep track of the contractions and how far apart they were coming. She informed us that the hospital some thirty-five miles away would be called to alert the medical staff that we were on our way. She provided them with the details of my condition.

No tears came because shock was settling in. The words of our nurse friend were replaying over in my mind, *"You are going to have this baby today. It is going to happen today."* My mind was going a hundred miles an hour with more questions than answers and some of them involved death. *"Would the baby live? Was it too early? Did the water breaking this soon mean suffocation? Would I get medical attention soon enough? Was the baby going to come while driving to the hospital some thirty-five miles away?"*

The questions stopped when another onset of pain began, it startled me back to reality. I remembered I was to keep track of how far apart the contractions were coming. They were so inconsistent I thought, *"Was I going crazy? Fifteen minutes, then five minutes, then ten minutes. What did this mean?"* The fear was back and setting in deep within me. I felt like I was in a daze and having an out of body experience. *"It all has to be a bad dream."* I was beginning to become numb to my surroundings.

My husband was driving very fast, close to ninety miles per hour, so fast I was closing my eyes and trying to remember to focus on timing how far apart the contractions were coming. We talked a little and glanced at each other every time more pain came. The reality of the baby arriving too early, was beginning to be planted in our minds, that he or she may not even live. We would then be left empty armed and wondering, *"Why God?"* We had waited so long for this baby.

We arrived! The drive took us twenty minutes, making it in nearly half the normal time it would take, it was 5:40 p.m. There were three or four nurses waiting outside the Emergency Room doors with a wheelchair. As soon as the pickup stopped the passenger side door was flung open and I was helped into the wheelchair and rushed away to the reality of a baby arriving seven weeks too early.

It was like a dream or a television show as I was being quickly rushed down the cool-feeling hallways to the emergency room while being asked all kinds of questions. I did not want to talk. This was all a bad dream. I felt myself leaving my body; like I was talking for another person. *"This could not be happening? It was a terrible nightmare."* The next hour would be etched in my mind forever.

They stripped my clothes off as fast as they could in exchange for a hospital gown. I was hooked up to all kinds of monitors and then they prepped me for a pelvic exam. Next, the ultra sound machine was being rolled in to see if they could view the baby to evaluate the situation. My husband was standing by my side trying to hold back his tears while the nurses were rushing around me like bees on honey. They all became extremely quiet and there still was no doctor present. The silence of the nurses is what brought emotions and tears rolling out of me. Up until this time, no tears had been released. What no parents ever wants to hear was said by a nurse, "I cannot find a heartbeat."

The tears broke like a wall of water being dammed up, I was sobbing and could not stop. The baby was possibly dead. Seven long months of waiting, not including the six years' prior of trying to get pregnant. This day was not supposed to be like this, I had anticipated a much different entrance into the world. Tears kept on coming from both of us. My husband was trying to hold and comfort me through the mess of wires and tubes from all the monitors and machines. No words, embrace, or touch would stop the numbness settling in and overtaking me. I was slowly moving into silence…until a nurse yelled, "I found it. I found the heartbeat!" Gasping from everyone's breath being held and sighs of relief is what was heard, not to mention the biggest smiles were on everyone's faces.

There was a heartbeat, the baby was alive! *"What next?"* *"Where was the doctor?"* This made me nervous. He was notified at the time the hospital was called, but he still had not arrived. It was Saturday night and, it turned out, he was a race car driver and was getting ready for the stock car races at the local track. Shortly after the nurse found the heartbeat he appeared and quickly took charge.

The doctor consulted with all the nurses to get the rundown on all that had transpired since I had entered the hospital. He reassured us that we were indeed going to be welcoming our baby into this world tonight. It was determined an emergency delivery was needed and the baby would come by cesarean. The eerie feeling came over me as I was rushed into a cold surgical room with more wires and monitors along with medicine being given to me. A white cloth was draped over me to block the view of the fast-approaching delivery process that was about to begin. Everyone was gowned up and ready to start, my husband included, he was right by my side.

Tears began streaming from my eyes again as I was having a hard time staying in the present moment. I was feeling no pain from where the incision was made because of the epidural I was given. I was told each step of the process as it was happening in a play by play blow. All I wanted to know was if the baby was okay and I wanted to hear a whimper, a cry, and to hear the doctor say, "The baby is alive!"

At 6:34 p.m. the loudest scream from a newborn was heard along with joyful congratulations from doctor and nurses. A baby boy! Our tears of sadness quickly turned to tears of joy. The baby was very much alive, he was screaming like crazy and had a full head of black hair. The nurses quickly took him away and had my husband come with while the doctor stitched me up from the surgery. They told me he was small, weighing four pounds, five and half ounces. Minutes later after he was being examined and observed, it was determined he was not breathing well enough on his own because of his underdeveloped lungs and would need more help than they could provide. He would need to be taken care of at a much larger, more equipped medical center for premature babies.

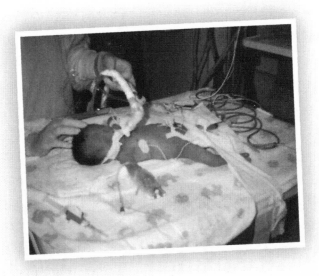

More questions were being hurled at me. Where did we prefer the baby to go? *"Go where? I had not even met him or held him and now he needed to be swept away?"* The air ambulance was notified in the city we lived in and would be arriving within a short time to take our new baby boy away from us.

The questions started again; what was our son's name, what were our full names, address, dates of birth? It was never ending. All I wanted to do was hold my baby. I only got a glimpse of him when he was screaming as he was lifted above the white cloth draped over my lower half. More questions, who would be flying with the baby and who would be staying with me? There were so many questions and no good answers. We were simply being carried by faith.

They moved me into a private room with nurses and doctor coming in and out asking more questions. They were constantly giving us the status of our baby and the estimated arrival of the air ambulance. *"It all seemed like make believe fairy tale. Maybe we would wake up from this horrible dream."*

All the questions had been answered; it was determined that my husband was staying with me to bring me home in a day or two after I was discharged, the motorcycle would be trailered back by our friends, and my mom would meet the air ambulance so there would be family with our son in case he did not make it through the night. This was too much to take in and I began to feel this out of body experience happen again. I was so scared that there were no emotions from me because the reality was so terrifying. I still had not seen my new baby so worry was beginning to take over my thoughts when suddenly the doors of my room

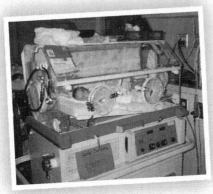

opened. In came so many people — nurses, doctors, personnel from the air ambulance team, and a gurney with an incubator on it and our baby boy.

My eyes were focused on him inside this plastic incubator lying on his stomach. I faintly heard one of the many medical personnel standing in this crowded room say, "We could spend only a few minutes with him. We need to leave soon." Everyone left the room and for the first time we were alone with our son. We looked at each other with tears in our eyes, not knowing what to do or say. I wanted so desperately to hold him; I had not even touched him. This was not how the ending of the story was supposed to happen. I held back the tears that would not stop because I needed to be the best, strong mom I could be at this moment.

"Was this really happening?" The doctor peeked his head into the room and said, "We have to leave soon." I looked at him with desperation and for direction, *"What was I to do or say to this little boy who was only a few hours old and being taken away?"* With the most kind, gentle eyes the

doctor looked at me and said, "Talk to him. Tell him you love him, that everything will be okay. Put your arm in this hole and touch him, stroke his arm, his back, and let him know you will be there and see him in a few days."

The long-awaited touch of our son was like stroking a small baby animal. He was so tiny and frail, he looked like a baby robin bird, weak and helpless. He felt warm and like the softest velvety material. His chest was moving up and down, but his breathing was labored. I spoke words of love and encouragement to say I would always be there for him no matter what happened. I told him to keep fighting and to stay around long enough for dad and me to hold him in our arms. As I was getting comfortable talking to him, the kind doctor entered and said, "We have to go."

At 10:30 p.m. the sound of the helicopter blades lifting the air ambulance off the roof of the hospital was the eeriest sound for parents to *hear. "The sound stays with a person for a life time."* Life given and life taken away — away by air ambulance. The life we had so patiently waited for may now be the last time we would see our precious baby boy. *"We truly were being carried by faith."*

By midnight, grandma had arrived to meet her first grandson. Being a registered nurse by trade she was used to high pressure, medical situations and well-prepared to be the family member to stand by our baby's side. She would encourage him to be strong and remind him to stay around long enough to have mom and dad meet up with him in a few days. He was not alone.

There was little sleep that crossed our eyes the rest of the night as the only thoughts were *"When was I getting out of the hospital to go home to be with my baby?"* The sleepless night passed slowly. In the early hours of the morning around 3:00 a.m. August 29th, there was a call from grandma telling us our son was in stable condition and the doctors were taking good care of him. These were the most comforting words we needed to hear, to know that grandma was staying close by him, making sure he was not alone.

REFLECTION PAUSE

Trying times! There is nothing as difficult in a life as contemplating losing a child. This experience made me think back over my life, to other difficult times...

Freedom from my parents! I was starting my life on my own, away from them, to prove I was not the teenage menace they feared. I left home the day of high school graduation to move one hundred miles away with my big city boyfriend and attend college to get a four-year degree in business. I planned on finding my way in the business world, making a lot of money, and becoming the "somebody" I so desperately wanted to be. I would show my parents, especially my dad, and everyone in the small town, I was going to be 100% different than the reckless teenager I had become.

The controlled pattern of drinking and drugging allowed me to be productive, keeping my grades at an average scale to stay on target to graduate from college and hold down the job to make money to pay off my student loan. Bound and determined to not be financially dependent on my parents or my husband I would pay it off in five years.

In this control stage of drinking it carried over to obsessively watching my husband's life of drinking and using. When control became my security blanket it was like a pair of magnifying glasses glued to my eyes. My attitude was that "I was better than everyone else because my life and drinking were under control." The person under the microscope was my husband. His drinking and using was out of control according to my new-found standards and something had to change.

My introduction to the twelve-step program, for those with alcohol problems, was through the back door. This was because I first attended the twelve-step program for family members of those who have alcohol issues. I believed I did not have the problem, my husband did. Yet, a strong forthright woman who was my sponsor in this program confronted my arrogant attitude and asked if I had ever looked at my own drinking and drug use issues. This was the first time I was smacked in the face with having to look at the true me.

Going through substance abuse treatment was the beginning of my life free of alcohol and drugs. In my crazy thinking, after treatment, I would totally be fixed and become a lovey, dovey, wonderful person once I put the plug in the jug. NOT! Well, I sure knew it would come true when I realized there were only twelve steps to work and I would have a new life. I would have them comfortably finished in one year, by doing one step per month. Then, in my mind, graduating and receiving a degree, and also figuring out how to continue this controlled drinking while eliminating the dire consequences. The magic wand was being waved over me, tah dah, everything would magically be better.

Reality set in when my husband wanted nothing to do with my grandiose plan. This created a deep wedge between us that was enough to have me thinking about divorce and getting rid of his sorry attitude. Once he decide to go to substance abuse treatment, things began to change. We both were working on ourselves and had nothing to do with our old friends, alcohol and drugs. We began to live a new way and this included learning about and believing in the idea of a Higher Power. Eventually I let this idea into my life to invade my mind with the new-found concept of prayer and meditation. I believe this, and the challenges from those women to pray, were what saved our marriage. God was showing me He was going to be in my life for the long haul.

Once I let God in, He was not moving out. This was the beginning of the walls crumbling around my heart and being penetrated by His love. I also was letting go of some of the control. I was examining myself and the behaviors that raised their ugly heads. Change was slow and at times not at all because stubbornness and being ornery were character defects I held onto like a security blanket.

In the process of working on my flaws, I had given in to my husband during a weak moment in the mending stage of our relationship, and then had to face the biggest fear of my life, being a mother. I believed I was not mothering material, that was given to the other women who appeared to have this warm, nurturing presence about them. I did love my husband and wanted to make him happy and maybe it would be kind of fun to have a person with the combination of both our personalities.

This change of heart, to become a mother, put a damper on my lofty corporate career plans. I was deep into "moving up the ladder" and this would potentially create a problem. There were many unwritten rules in the business world on women balancing the mothering game. The strength needed to carry many responsibilities and not become weak was a constant gnaw on my mind.

One perceived item of weakness of being a mother was how much time was needed to allocate to your children. The undefined line of how much was too much always existed. May it be time on the phone with children or their caretakers or time attending

activities and events. It seemed like the more author-
ity and responsibility I gained, the less time I could
allocate. All along I thought, once I reached a higher
level of management I would have more freedoms and
flexibility with my children.

Many women can do it all; climb and fight to get
to the top of their careers and handle the responsibil-
ities with children while not letting it interfere with
the corporate work environment. I could do it for a
few years, but there was a constant gnawing in my
entire belief system about what my true role in my
life was to be.

One child later and I had a whole different world
open to me. This new person, our son, came from a
small cell of two separate individuals, formed in my
womb and now making me analyze the entire way
I lived, thought, and valued life. This love was inde-
scribable and my corporate, self-centered, focused
world was turned upside down and inside out. Priori-
ties changed and I viewed my life very differently. The
focus of my career was being changed in my heart and
I needed to find a way I could handle all that was in
front of me. I was coming to realize how God highly
values the faithfulness of women being mothers, and
that they have a very powerful and influential job in
this world.

Trying to Be Somebody Years

[MY THIRTIES]

 This is what I REMEMBER from this time IN MY LIFE...

Motherhood vs. Corporatehood

Our early arrival baby was very weak and needed a lot of medical attention. He remained in the hospital for three weeks and was released with a high-risk status. We had the option to take him home with monitors to keep a constant watch on him to ensure he was breathing and staying with us or not to have them. Our choice was to not have them because we felt if he was going to die and be taken away from us we would rather that he goes peacefully in his sleep, and without us stressing over the monitors buzzing and screeching and us not knowing what to do.

I took an extended maternity leave because of the emergency C-section birth and to take care of a high-risk baby. Being several weeks early, this meant I was not able to tie up all the loose ends at work like I had planned prior to his birth. There was nothing I could do about the situation, we were now talking about life or death with a new baby boy in our lives. Things were changing in my heart with my work priorities being of lower importance.

What mattered now was this little baby boy lying in an incubator with wires taped all over his body, looking so weak, helpless, and at times lifeless. I made it back home in two days after his birth to finally be with him. He was so small and frail looking, but he was a fighter. I so badly wanted to hold him and whisper in his ear how much I loved him and that he was born to fight and grow to be

a strong man. My heart was breaking inside because I was not able to hold him until he was stable. He was seven days old when we got to put him in our arms. It was not the normal picture of mom and dad cuddling their newborn, it was an event of nurses delicately placing him in our arms. Wires were part of the cuddling and we only could hold him for very short periods of time because he needed to be placed back in the incubator. For the next three weeks I was by his side every minute of the day talking and touching him as much as possible. He needed to know I was there and he was my new focus.

Once our baby was healthier and we had him settled into daycare, I got back to the corporate world. I told myself, "*It will be okay. I was successful in my career. How difficult could it be to add one little child into the mix of this life?*" The love of a child, with no words spoken, and the look of innocent eyes would drive a wedge in my heart between him and work. My baby was depending on me to help him live and before this no one had counted on me in this way.

Sobriety, parenting, marriage, and career were the most challenging events I had ever tackled up to this time in my life. Trying to balance all of them was like an analogy of a plate twirler trying to keep several plates spinning all at one time on thin poles with none of them dropping and crashing to the floor. As with a plate twirler, it seemed like a continual race of running back and forth trying to keep all the responsibilities going, spinning, without having it all crash in front of me. Stress described best the anxiousness felt when I kept the fast pace going that was required to maintain everything in perfect balance. It was beginning to take a toll on me and I was questioning, "*How am I going to deal with all these challenges coming at me all at once?*"

My old coping skills of drinking and drugging were not an option anymore, especially now with a child to raise.

From what I was being taught, I guessed I was to work on talking to God and having Him help me in what felt like a hopeless situation. I had come to know this loving God, but I did not let Him in as an active part of these challenges. It was confusing, overwhelming, and fearful. *"If He loved me so much, why was all this happening? Was I being carried by faith?"*

This relationship with God was difficult to grasp. I was still hiding from God because I did not feel worthy and good enough for Him. I was attending church and meeting many wonderful people who were helping me understand the love God had for me and the forgiveness He offered. They did not know the dark past I had come from and it was not forgivable in my eyes. This kept me miserable and hiding with shame for a long time. Life would have to go on, it had become much better than it was in the past. I could live with my thoughts of *"God could not forgive me."*

For three years, life continued down a path of work, parenting, marriage, and trying to stay clean and sober. Church became a large part of my life while the twelve-step meetings took a backseat because it was too challenging to make time to get to meetings. I was getting plugged into small group meetings offered at church and embarked on a journey to learn about the Bible, prayer, and God's love. There were many wonderful women who came alongside me to help answer my questions, to teach me how to pray, and give me hope that God had forgiven me and truly had a purpose for my life, *"Even though I highly doubted it."* My dark past was painful and full of shame too unspeakable to be forgiven, let alone to think God had a plan for my life. I was satisfied at this point in my life with all the good things that had happened to me. It was much better than I had ever dreamed of, I was okay with where it was. Life would go on.

New Pastime

Being clean and sober, my husband and I needed a new activity to keep us busy, so we decided riding motorcycle would be fun. Our first motorcycle was a 1992 Harley Davidson 1200cc Sportster. We rode whenever free time presented itself, putting thousands of miles on the odometer and meeting many new friends.

After being the passenger for several years, and not to mention a well-seasoned back seat driver, I had had enough of riding behind my husband and we purchased a second Harley, a 1993 Dyna Wide Glide, which became his. I then took command of the Sportster.

It had been years since I had driven my own motorcycle. I had been twelve years old and learned on an 80cc dirt bike. Other women riders I met suggested taking a motorcycle safety instructional course before getting my license, especially when I would now have control over such a large motorcycle. It was a huge commitment to spend four hours every evening for a week in class but I hoped it was well worth the time and effort. The goal was to leave the class more comfortable and confident.

As parents, we determined that riding motorcycle would be a family affair. We continued to ride as frequently as new parents could with a young child. Involving our son was a must since he was born at a motorcycle rally. At a very young age, he began riding on his dad's lap during short rides, he loved it and always wanted to go. On long rides, we left him behind with our parents.

Most years we took a trip to the Sturgis Bike Rally in the Black Hills of South Dakota. We loved riding in the beautiful scenery and enjoyed the time with our friends. It was hard to leave our son, but our parents were wonderful for taking care of him for a few days while we were gone. One year a story unfolded that will be forever etched in our memories.

Motorcycle Miracle

My motorcycle is jerking side to side, I see smoke billowing out of the RV right in front of me. I later learned the smoke was from the engine exploding and spewing oil and anti-freeze over the blacktop of the highway. Since I was the first motorcycle behind the RV, I hit the oil and antifreeze slick, which was more slippery than ice, and sent my bike and me into an out of control tail spin.

My mind raced with these thoughts, *"I know the end is coming quick. I cannot believe it is all going to end somewhere along Interstate between Rapid City and Sturgis, South Dakota. My husband and my son."* I remembered having just passed the veteran's cemetery, and prayed I would not become one of the motorcycle accident statistics of the 1996 Bike Rally. At that second, the strangest thing happened, the voice of my motorcycle safety instructor, whom I had listened to for close to forty hours during the training a few years before, spoke clearly in my mind: *"Don't fight it; lay it down. Don't fight it; lay it down!"* During the training when he said those words, they made no sense. Now, in the moment of impending disaster, it made perfect sense! I had no other choice. I had to do something because destruction was ready to happen. The likelihood of me getting out of this situation alive was low, so I thought, *"I might as well lay the bike down. I had no other option."* A total wreck would be happening soon, it was inevitable. Consciously I shifted my weight to the right side and pulled the entire motorcycle over. I started going down and a million thoughts flashed in my mind, *"I did not want my life to end. I had found God and He cleaned me up. He set me on a new path with a loving husband and an incredible, active son. Life could not end. I wanted to live!"*

Those thoughts quickly shifted when I realized I was still alive! One second everything changed. When I released my bike, I had been spun 180 degrees and now facing oncoming traffic. My motorcycle was gone, and now it was only me and the highway. I am sliding down the Interstate on my backside on the oil and antifreeze mixture. The only protection between the black top and myself was my leather vest, jeans, and riding boots. I had taken my helmet and leather jacket off and strapped them on the back of the bike.

The fast racing Interstate traffic that I was riding with in a smooth flowing rhythm is now coming straight for me. I felt like a steel ball in a pinball machine not knowing what direction or what I would hit next. Still sliding at speeds exceeding sixty miles per hour, my body was like limp spaghetti; feet in the air, arms flailing, while I am trying to hold my head off the pavement. It was imperative for me to keep my head lifted so I could attempt to see what might happen next. I steadied my head and saw the next obstacle right in front of me, another Harley. It was a lone machine that had thrown its riders off and was ready to take me out. This unmanned metal giant and I were about to collide. *"How was I still alive?"*

I might make it out of this terrifying event if I am not smashed by the huge chunk of metal coming straight for me. Being in this dangerous position with my legs sprawled out, I see the Harley lying on its side, and the hand bars are aimed directly at my groin area. I instantly pull my legs together and draw my knees into my chest to get myself into a tight tuck position. I am in a form of a ball with my head lifted and legs together, and my riding boots are acting as the only additional protection between my body and the oncoming Harley. I aim my feet for the seat of the fast-approaching motorcycle with hopes to have my boots connect with the seat and miss the handle bars altogether. BAM...JOLT...PRESSURE. I feel the intense impact when my boots hit the center of the seat. The forceful collision has such tremendous power and is like a pommel horse in gymnastics and it shoots me off the seat and propels me into the air. While traveling mid-air, I complete two full somersaults and am like a professional gymnast waiting for the perfect landing. BANG…THUD…HIT. Both feet land squarely in a tight formation as I land in a standing position on the shoulder of the Interstate. *"I AM STAND-ING. Yes! I AM STANDING!"* I am facing the ditch, looking at houses and the beautiful hillside in the Black Hills of South Dakota. I was alive! *"Or was I? If it was Heaven it sure looked a lot like Sturgis!"* After I collected my thoughts, I realized I was alive and not in Heaven. Since I was still here, I figured I had to be hurt and bloody after surviving that crazy ride!

My attention is drawn away from the houses and hill-side as I begin to look downward and begin to thoroughly examine my body, which must be a mangled, bloody mess. I start with my mid-section; *"My vest is still on and snapped."* I looked down farther to my legs; *"My jeans are still intact, apart from a small tear in the knee on the right pant leg."* *"Okay, this is good."* Now, for the feet, *"My boots are still on my feet."* And my arms, *"They had to be full of road rash from all the crazy positions and angles my body had just endured. My leather jacket sure would have come in handy."* Looking at both arms individually, *"The left one was fine, absolutely nothing wrong, no broken skin, no blood, no road rash."* The right arm, *"Close to the same as the left except for a small break of skin with a trace of blood oozing out, but noth-ing more than I had ever experienced from years of growing up on the farm."* I begin moving a bit to see if there is any pain to indicate broken bones — there was nothing! Absolutely nothing seems to be wrong with me!

Our friends escaped all this action by quickly pulling off to the shoulder of the Interstate to get out of harm's way. They were the first people to run up to me mere seconds after I landed. They witnessed the entire incident and could not believe I was standing. They made me sit down and began looking me over. They too found nothing wrong with me, absolutely nothing. I started to shake it off, *"I was truly carried by faith."*

Reality began to set in and my thoughts were clearing when two men approached me, saying, "We are off duty EMTs and want to examine you to make sure you are okay." They begin the exam by first looking in my eyes, and asking a few questions, "What day it is? Where are you? What just happened?" I answered all the questions and told them, "There is nothing wrong with me. I just looked myself over, and there is truly nothing wrong!" They looked at each other and back at me with amazement and said, "You are right. We cannot see anything wrong with you."

In astonishment, the EMT's moved on to the man and woman who were thrown from their motorcycle, the same motorcycle I jarred with minutes before. They were lying in the ditch and were told not to move with what seemed to be serious injuries while the ambulance was called along with other emergency personnel beginning to arrive. There were so many things happening all at once, it was a blur of activity.

The driver from the RV and his wife came running to me in disbelief of what had just transpired behind them in the short seconds after noticing their RV was not running correctly. They apologized profusely for the situation that had happened and were then speechless as they looked at what was before their eyes; a man and woman lying in the ditch, me standing with my friends trying to figure out where my motorcycle was, and tons of other spectators who had stopped because the Interstate was covered with all types of debris, oil, and antifreeze. There were also all sorts of vehicles and motorcycles frozen in their last location from trying to avoid becoming part of this disaster.

My only thought after experiencing chaos, *"I have had enough action for the day and I am ready to get out of here."* I looked at my friends and said, "Did you see where my motorcycle landed?" No, they had not noticed because their eyes were glued on watching me slide down the Interstate and then fly in the air doing somersaults while the whole time praying to not witness my death. As my friend would describe the story for years, she watched my face and my eyes and saw death pass through me. It was hard on her as she had many night-mares for some time.

What startled me out of my dazed thoughts were the loud shouts from surrounding people yelling to the man and woman from the RV saying, "The RV is on fire!" They ran back some 100 feet or more to the disabled motionless RV, and up the steps to gain access to their personal items. The next thing you could see were items from the RV being chucked into the ditch in hopes to escape its doomed fiery inferno that was bound to happen in a few short minutes. Clothes, coolers, bedding, bags, it all was landing in the ditch. What you heard next was many people simultane-ously yelling, "It is going to blow. Get back, get back!" Just like an action thriller movie, the RV exploded; BANG... BOOM...ROAR! There was black smoke, red hot flames, and people running away from the fire and the smoke. It was so intense and it looked like a mini atomic bomb going off. Within minutes the RV was engulfed in flames and burning rapidly. It burned down so all you could see was the skeletal metal framework. After watching this action, I was thinking, *"What could possibly happen next? When is this going to end?"*

The South Dakota Highway Patrol had been on scene for a few minutes and began blocking all traffic. The accident was unbelievable; smoke and fire continuing to come from the RV with fire trucks madly rushing to contain the blaze so it would not take off into the dry foliage of the ditches. The officers begin to assess the scene by blocking all westbound traffic to allow clean-up of the oil and antifreeze that saturated the Interstate and to begin interviewing and questioning all drivers and witnesses to collect the details. *"Wow. How do I describe what happened? There are no words to give it justice."* Facts, it must be factual words that come out of my mouth. Second by second, I account the last half hour of my life. While detailing the events out loud, my mind is wondering, *"What just happened? I am still alive. How can it be? I knew I was carried by faith."*

As my friends stand by my side they fill in the gaps of the story from their vantage point since they were pulled off to the shoulder of the Interstate. As crazy as it may seem, my friend whipped out her camera and began taking pictures of this unbelievable circumstance. I thought, *"She is crazy to be taking pictures."* Her quick reaction of snapping photos would be the images I looked back on to see all the details of this unbelievable story.

After standing on the shoulder of the highway for what felt like a lifetime I realized, *"I was not hurt. The fire was being contained. The injured riders were being loaded into the ambulance."* I said to my friends, "Where is my motorcycle? And where is my husband?" I was ready to leave because there was nothing left we could do. I had been examined by EMT's, interviewed by the highway patrol, and we were standing in the middle of the Interstate looking at each other. I was thinking, *"I rode here on my motorcycle and that will be the only way I get out of here. I hoped my motorcycle was crumbled in a big ball of metal and would need to be hauled away."* We surely could not ride three people on our friends' Harley, but I could ride on the back of my husband's motorcycle, *"Where was he?"*

When my husband passed the RV, he had noticed that the traffic thinned out behind him so he decided to pull off to the shoulder of the road and wait for us. He was located about two miles ahead of where the accident happened, but the layout of the road was such that there was a curve in the Interstate and it blocked his view of where the accident had taken place. After waiting for what seemed like an eternity and noticing no traffic on the highway, he become worried. He did not know what to do when a stranger in a car stopped to tell him there was a very bad motorcycle accident back a ways and there were a few motorcycles down and a lot of emergency vehicles.

Immediately he got on his bike, went down through the median and began driving towards the accident scene. The view that no one wants to witness was right in front of him: fire and smoke, tons of emergency vehicles; fire trucks, ambulances, highway patrol and rescue vehicles, and all traffic being blocked with two motorcycles down. He stopped his motorcycle and frantically began looking for me and our friends. It was difficult to find us with so many people and vehicles to sort through, and he began to think the worst because of the chaotic scene. Panic sets in and his life passes in front of him; his wife and two friends are in bad shape or dead, what would he tell his son and their children?

At the same time he is looking for us, we see him searching and somewhat trotting and then he takes off in a full-paced run right towards me. Our embrace was kind of like a fairy tale ending with him grabbing me firmly to assure himself I was really in his arms, then he began to hug and kiss my face. He finally stepped back while taking a hold of my shoulders and looked me in the eyes and said, "You are alive!" Like many others had done in the last half hour, he examined me to make sure I was okay. My response was simple and frustrating to him, "Yes, I am fine. Did you see my bike?" I was numb to what was happening and wanted to get out of this situation. Little did he know what had just taken place over the last thirty minutes. By this time, I had had enough of the whole scene — sliding down the Interstate at seventy miles per hour, being launched into the weirdest positions, landing on the side of the ditch, an exploding RV, EMTs poking me, and the reality of still being alive was enough for this tough girl!

After a few times of all of us saying, "Oh my goodness. What are we going to do now?" we made the decision to search for my motorcycle. It did not take us too long to find it. Silently, I was hoping it would be twisted, mangled, and totaled and the only hope of getting it home would be by trailer. At that very minute, I had no intentions of *ever* riding a motorcycle again.

Looking for my motorcycle was another reality check for me as the one who had just survived such a crazy accident. We walked on the blacktop of the Interstate following the trail of oil and antifreeze that spread over the entire lane for a long distance to find my motorcycle on the opposite side of the lane. It lay there looking somewhat normal, its true condition was like me, very little damage. There were only a few scrape marks on the right front brake lever and the back tail-light. The most obvious damage was on the front-end crash bars, which sustained moderate marks of shaved off metal. As I had left them, my leather jacket, helmet, and luggage bag were still securely strapped to the back of my motorcycle. The devastation of the whole ordeal started to sink in along with the huge amount of damage I escaped and most of all that my life had not ended.

Amazed at what we were witnessing in this metal horse, I internally hoped it would be flooded and would not start. But I knew that it was in good enough condition to ride and if it started, I would be forced to drive it home. After we picked it up, it was stabilized and checked over, the start button was engaged. To our astonishment one crank of the engine and it fired up! As the saying goes, "If you crash you have to get on and ride again." Ride I did, right into Sturgis. The short distance was extremely difficult because of how fearful I was of driving and how bad I was shaking. The entire way my eyes were filled with tears, yet I was so grateful, I was in disbelief that I was simply alive and able to ride away from one of the most traumatic events in my life.

Once we arrived in Sturgis we went straight to our central gathering place where we would meet friends every day. It would be quite the riding story to share for the day. As we talked about what happened, people gathered around to hear us describing the details of the accident. Most people were saying they already heard about it because the Interstate was closed and the news of a motorcycle accident during Sturgis always brings lots of discussion amongst bikers.

As late afternoon arrived with plenty of talking and sharing of the amazement of the horrific accident it was like I was talking about another person, not myself. While telling others about the details of this action-packed event, it was like retelling a fiction story, exhilarating to describe and wondering how it all ended. When the day came to an end, the excitement wore off and it was time to head back to our hotel in Deadwood, South Dakota; which is accessed by Canyon Road, one of the curviest and dangerous twenty-mile rides in the Black Hills. The ride would be terrifying now that it was evening and dark outside. I was more scared than ever, yet, I knew I had to conquer this fear and get on and ride. I was ready to meet my demons. I suited up with my full gear by putting on my jacket, helmet, and goggles. The normal ride takes about twenty minutes, this felt like eternity, even though it was only around thirty minutes.

When we arrived, I was so relieved and never happier to get to the hotel. I cried the entire way and could barely see at times from the non-stop stream of tears.

It was hard to collect my emotions and settle myself down. I was anxious, in shock, and not sure if I wanted to try and sleep. Rest would not come easy. My mind began questioning itself, *"Maybe it all was a crazy dream."* As I lay in bed trying to sleep, the entire day unfolded with each grave detail of the accident rolling around in my head; the sights, sounds, people, feelings, the emotions — it was overwhelming to process. Reliving every second of the accident, the moment when my life flashed in front of my eyes kept spinning wildly in my mind the entire night. *"How did I decide to lay the bike down? How did my head not touch the pavement? How did I connect so perfectly with the oncoming motorcycle? How many somersaults did I do? Why did I have no injuries? How come the RV exploded? How could my motorcycle have so little damage? How could I be alive?"* It made no sense and was too much to wrap my mind around. I tried to redirect my thoughts to the present moment and what I knew about myself. I knew that I easily bruised and surely would wake up with injuries along with black and blue marks all over my body. My neck would be stiff and I would need to get checked over by a doctor. I continued to stare into the darkness unable to find sleep, repeatedly wondering, *"How had I lived through this ordeal and why was I alive?"* This God I let into my life a few years back seemed to be part of the answer. He had truly performed a miracle on my behalf and must want me to do something with my life. *"He was carrying me."*

I closed my eyes to rest and then a vision of an image flashed in my mind just as quickly as the accident happened and I saw a little cherubim angel with long brown hair. I knew God was allowing me to begin to see into the spiritual realm and I realized how real He truly was, more than I had ever admitted. *"He was carrying me."*

Rest finally came to me. When I awoke the next morning, I was alive and to my astonishment I did not have one bruise, black and blue mark, or stiff neck. It was a miracle! *"A motorcycle miracle."* Exhilarated with a new realization of what God had done for me the excitement and joy were pouring out and I had a fantastic idea to show how much God was alive and in me. I was bound and determined to go through with my idea.

I dashed out of our room to wake my friend so she could be my partner in the plan. I needed her because I knew as soon as my husband found out what I was scheming he would know I was off my rocker. My idea — I was getting a tattoo! My friend, of course, thought it was a great plan, so much that she would get her old tattoo brightened up and we would both have something to talk about when we got home. We then informed our husbands of the plan.

It may have seemed like it would be a quick project to get accomplished, however it took close to a half a day. Why? We needed to find a clean tattoo artist, especially one who could draw the cherubim angel as I was picturing it in my mind. The guy we found was quite interesting, he had body piercings and tattoos everywhere and this was before it was common. He had drawn the angel perfectly, exactly how I could imagine it. The cherubim angel with long brown hair was tattooed on my left shoulder with the words, "Carried by Faith." The process took about one hour and my friend continued to capture the whole ordeal with pictures. This was proof I was there and that all of this did truly happen.

As for the cherubim angel I saw in the middle of the night, I believe God revealed to me that this angel was sent from Him with a loud whistle blown and saying, *"Go down and get her. Swoop her up and do not let one bone be broken. Nor one bruise be on her body. Set her down gently on the shoulder of the road. This way she can see that I chose to carry her to safety. She needs to stay here on earth and help others by telling about this amazing miracle!"* Whenever the story is told people are in awe and disbelief. In our rational minds there is absolutely no reason I am alive.

I continued in a state of conscious awareness and reverence for God and His miraculous work for many weeks, months, and years. The lasting imprint is my tattoo that I look at every morning to remind me how I was "Carried by Faith" by an angel on that very hot day in Sturgis back in 1996.

For he will command his angels concerning you
to guard you in all your ways; they will lift you up
in their hands, so that you will not
strike your foot against a stone.

[PSALM 91:11-12 NIV]

REFLECTION PAUSE

My career was everything and at times, more important than family. I continued to work hard in my corporate job to prove to myself and others I "was somebody." Life as I knew it was turned upside down and inside out by this beautiful baby God allowed to enter our lives. Those years will go down as some of the most self-discovering, rewarding, and revealing times. I was coming into a true understanding of myself with my many flaws and character defects and realizing how much I needed to work on me and being a parent so I could be the best mom possible.

The dependence on alcohol and drugs had been removed, yet terrible outbursts of anger and untamed emotions were always bubbling at my surface. I continued to hate myself and the many things from my past. I recognized how they left huge scars on my life. I was determined to improve myself by looking at the past hurts and having the courage to change so I could start feeling better.

Since God was now a part of my life I immersed myself in the Bible, any good Christian book, church services, spiritual conferences, worship music, and speakers to try to become full of this new way of living. I was beginning to understand how God was shaping my life and I was feeling more filled up than empty.

My faith prior to the motorcycle accident was weak. Believing I was forgiven to a point, for my little sins, but not sure about all the big ones. I was going to church and feeling God's presence, especially during the worship music. Reading the Bible was challenging and hard to understand, BUT, there was always this big BUT. I was not one hundred percent convinced that God truly loved me. It was impossible to believe He had forgiven me for all the dark years of my past, and that He could do something special in my life.

BUT — after the motorcycle miracle there was no doubt in my mind God loved me like I was the only one. He cared about every little detail of my life. Everything was new after the accident as I looked at life through a clearer lens. My sobriety and twelve-step program was more alive and interesting. My faith in God deepened and I wanted to dive into knowing God on a new level. My passion for life and gratitude for being alive ignited my desire to know God in a whole different way. I needed and wanted to change more of my behaviors, actions, and attitudes.

I was being taught that Jesus was a real person, He came to show us deep love and forgiveness. This is not just for me, but all of us. He was willing to die for us so that we could be set free of all our past mistakes. Jesus lived and died so we could live a free life in God's Kingdom. He was put to death on a cross and resurrected to show that He is alive today in our lives through the Holy Spirit.

The act of love Jesus showed and suffered through for me and you are unbelievable. He endured verbal ridicule, physical beatings, and an agonizing death. When we can get a glimpse of this and try to understand the cruelty and pain He suffered, it makes my heart be filled with huge amounts of sorrow. I feel sorry for my sins, all my actions that hurt God. To have turned my back on Him, the true love I was searching for all my life, is difficult to understand.

I had to fully concede and ask Jesus into my life, to take away the wreckage of the past, to ask Him to come, and live in my heart to make me a new person. The Bible says it like this,

> If you confess with your mouth that
> Jesus is Lord and believe in your heart
> that God raised him from the dead,
> you will be saved.
>
> [ROMANS 10:9 NLT]

I was willing to ask Jesus into my life and have Him come and live in my heart. Every day since the first time I did it, I say something like this, "God, I have done wrong things in the past and have lived apart from you. I want to be forgiven for these mistakes, for any mistakes I have made recently and any I will make in the future. I believe Jesus died on the cross for me and rose again. God, I give you my life to do with it what you wish. Come into my life and live in my heart. In Jesus name. Amen."

This is how I found freedom *to be the person God intended ME to BE, boldly saying, "I need to BE okay being ME, the ME God intended ME to BE." It is stated best in the Bible,*

God made my life complete when I placed
all the pieces before him. When I got my act
together, He gave me a fresh start. Now I'm alert
to God's ways; I don't take God for granted.
Every day I review the ways He works;
I try not to miss a trick. I feel put back together,
and I'm watching my step. God rewrote the text
of my life when I opened the book
of my heart to His eyes.

[PSALM 18:20-24 MSG]

God sent the guardian angel down to take all the bruises and broken bones for me and leave me untouched. Therefore, the angel and words "Carried by Faith" are tattooed on my left shoulder above my heart to be a visible reminder of my faith in God, and how He has carried me through my life.

EPILOGUE

Many amazing adventures have happened in our journey of life since 1996 and the motorcycle miracle. We have been blessed with a second son in 1998 and now they are both grown men beginning to live their own lives. I am still blessed to be married to the big city boyfriend having recently celebrated thirty years of marriage in 2017.

My relationship with my parents is good. We frequently talk and have moved past the messy wreckage of my teenage past.

I have made a career change to be under God's management by trying to hear His still small voice and be willing to do whatever He has for me on any given day. As a professional speaker and author, I can express my passion of encouraging women to be the true person God intended them to be. I love talking and sharing about my ideas with others on how I keep trudging the road to a happy destiny.

Of course, the story does not end here. It continues to be written. The ending to this story is — there is no ending! With God present in my every waking moment, my life story never ends. There are only pauses and rests to reflect and be refreshed. He has too many things for me to accomplish before He takes me home. I was given life by God and I plan to use every minute to help others to know He can do for you, as He did for me! Set me *free*! He will always Carry Me by Faith.

Made in the USA
Lexington, KY
29 April 2018